The
OCCULT CAUSES
of the
PRESENT WAR

"In this work the author reveals the nature and existence of the hidden powers at work behind the Nazi organization, which he believes, is but the outward though appropriate, manifestation of satanist & diabolic agencies which employ it for their own malignant purposes." Satanic element in Naziism; Satanic power in old Germany; Witchcraft, satanism & the Vehmgerichte; Satanic power in modern Germany; Nazi pagan doctrine & church; Nazism & satanism.

Lewis Spence

ISBN 0-7661-0051-0

THE OCCULT CAUSES
OF THE PRESENT WAR

By
LEWIS SPENCE

3RD IMPRESSION

RIDER & CO.
LONDON : NEW YORK : MELBOURNE
47, Princes Gate, London, S.W.7

MADE AND PRINTED IN GREAT BRITAIN
AT GAINSBOROUGH PRESS, ST. ALBANS,
BY FISHER, KNIGHT & CO., LTD.

CONTENTS

CHAPTER I

CHAPTER IV

CHAPTER V

CHAPTER VI

CHAPTER VII

CHAPTER VIII

FOREWORD

THE majority of British people are at no loss to apportion the blame in assessing the causes of the present conflict. They accuse one man, Adolf Hitler, as the prime instigator of the catastrophe, and with perfect justice. In my view, however, the Führer is merely the creature and instrument of forces which for centuries have been making use of this or that dictator, tyrant, or other puppet notoriety to further their own arcane intentions, which, in a word, are the creation of general chaos and the final destruction of humanity.

One is well aware that 'as much and more has been said before,' only, I am afraid, it has not been said in a popularly acceptable manner. And even had it been put on record a hundred times, so shallow is popular memory that it seems vitally necessary to repeat it at a juncture in history when so much depends on probing to the radical causes of human unrest.

Quite a number of ostensible causes are cited by this writer or that as the true reasons for the outbreak of the Second Great War, conditions economic, racial, or merely the desire for retribution being advanced as the prime factors in its precipitation. Not one, but all of these may well rank as among its contributory causes.

It was when I began to study the strange phenomenon of a religious revolution in Nazi Germany that I believed I had found the clue to the character of the real forces behind the Nazi Party, and the true cause of the War. I had long ago been struck with the circumstance that practically every revolution of any consequence in Europe for centuries past had been accompanied by a very definite intention on the part of its creators either to sweep away the Christian Faith, or so deface and alter it as to render it unrecognizable. So it was in the France of the Revolution, so in Russia, in Spain, in Portugal, and so it now is in Nazi Germany.

It seemed to me strange and illogical that outbreaks ostensibly brought about through social unrest and racial, political, or economic causes should invariably vent upon religion and all its insignia the first uprush of their fury. With the political structure they were bent upon destroying they usually dealt more or less drastically, though by no means in all cases. But toward Christianity they behaved with a barbarous ferocity which far ourstripped any hatred they evinced for any political régime. And, no matter what the type of government they assailed, whether monarchist or republican, the sacrilegious nature of their attitude to the native Churches of the soil was still the same, even although it was not shared by the people of the country.

Nazi Germany now frankly declares herself as 'heathen,' and metes out the same persecution to Lutheran Protestants and Roman Catholics as she does to the Jewish Synagogue. The elements of rebellion in most revolutionary uprisings have pretended to see in Christianity one of the pillars of tyranny. But could this be said of the German Churches of both confessions? Assuredly it could not.

To account for this phenomenon one was logically compelled to seek for an organization in which a deep-seated hatred of the Christian Faith was the active principle. There could only be one such organization—that mysterious and well-concealed body of Satanist or Luciferian origin which has manifested itself in the case of practically every European revolt since the beginning of the Christian Era, and which has always attempted under the cloak of economic or political confusion to further its grand aim—the destruction of the Christian religion and the abasement of mankind.

This, then, is the thesis of this book. I could readily have extended the proof fourfold, but present exigencies make such a course impossible. In any case, I think I have afforded a sufficiency of evidence to prove my case and to reveal once again the existence of the gravest peril possible to humanity.

Unless that peril is sought out in its secret lairs by the

governments of the more responsible powers it will certainly continue to afflict and menace the peoples of Europe, to bring about ever-recurring wars and revolts, and to lie as a festering sore at the life-centres of European society. Surely the problem calls for the active participation of the leaders of European thought at the close of the present struggle, in order that the discovery of its nucleus and the extirpation of its malignant sodality may be accomplished, so that suffering humanity may be liberated from the incessant persecution of its insane and disastrous machinations.

L. S.

CHAPTER I

THE SATANIC ELEMENT IN NAZISM

IN his imperial hermitage at Doorn, Wilhelm Hohen-zollern, ex-Kaiser of Germany, has discovered a pastime equally intriguing with the craft of the forester to beguile the long hours of his leisure. He is known to spend the greater part of his time in the privacy of his princely library, much as did the first Napoleon in his book-panelled retreat at Longwood. A privileged literary visitor, how-ever, might well express surprise at the nature of the volumes which appear on its shelves, for instead of the titles on statesmanship and high politics, the historical folios, and the classical Aldines and Elzevirs which might appro-priately plenish the book-cases of majesty in retirement, he would find there works of one particular class only—books on the occult and the arcane.

It would soon become apparent to such a guest that the ex-Kaiser's librarian must have ransacked the bookshops of Leipsic, Paris, and London for works on the subject of secret societies, but, as these are comparatively rare, they occupy only a few shelves of the royal 'den.' Works upon Continental Freemasonry are much more in evidence, and, indeed, form the bulk of the collection, while volumes on the older arcane societies, the Vehmgerichte and the Illuminati, and on the mysterious cult of Lucifer, go to make up an accumulation of arcaner eference which seems the answer to the prayer of a dealer in occult literature.

As those privileged to enjoy the hospitality of the Kaiser's country seat are not permitted by etiquette to put the question direct to its master, it is not possible for them to inquire the reason for a literary preference rather unusual in royalty. It is, however, unnecessary to interrogate anyone on the point, for the answer is already known to quite a number of people. No man knows better than the astute and experienced gentleman who once ruled the destinies of sixty millions of Germans how he came to be deprived of his sovereignty—none is better aware of the true nature of the forces which beguiled him to risk his throne among the hazards of an evilly inspired conflict.

If any of his ministers had suggested to the Kaiser in the days before the Great War that hidden and destructive forces of malign and Satanic character might, for their own destructive ends, hurry him into war, he would certainly not have regarded it, as would some people of superior sapience, as a rather feeble joke. The quite extraordinary experiences of ruling princes and great statesmen give them to realize that in international politics there are more things than those which find expression in the philosophy of governments. He would probably have shared the view, often privately expressed, of the French, Austrian, and Russian rulers and premiers of that time that such a contingency was by no means remote. But in the fullness of his power and the security of a great nation in arms, he would as certainly have rejected as absurd the bare notion that ambushed and mysterious agencies of unknown captaincy could so misdirect and confuse his designs as to bring about his defeat and the consequent ruin of his empire.

Few, indeed, would have been the men of common sense who would have disagreed with him. But, alas, common sense, when dealing with matters so unusual and so obscure, is a poor substitute for uncommon sense, and the credulity of incredulity affords, perhaps, the best culture-bed for the germ of malign purpose.

So, in advanced old age, the ex-Emperor of Germany seeks tirelessly in the pages of mystical books for those clues and traces which may guide him to a more precise understanding of the forces which not only seduced him into war, but, by reason of their own inherent defects and furious irrationalities, betrayed him into defeat and exile. Every work published which might seem to aid him in his quest is studiously scanned in the hope that it will cast some light, however vague, upon the identity of those hidden leaders of a secret and occult junta, who, he is convinced, were responsible for the calamity of 1914 and the debacle of 1918.

But it is not in the pages of printed books that he may

find the key to the mystery of his undoing. The ministers of evil are much too skilfully versed in the arts of anonymity to leave their psychological finger-prints on the margins of current literature.

And what happened to the disfranchised Majesty of Doorn will as surely happen in due course to his fated successor, Adolf Hitler, who is, in every sense, an instrument much more typical of the choice of powers malign, and much more appropriate to their purposes than ever was Wilhelm the Second. He appears, indeed, nay, certainly is, a Faust of the sovereign preference of Lucifer himself, a tool so utterly significant of evil intention as to be revealed as the grand dupe of the Satanic purpose for all time. It is notorious among the inquirers into Satanic history and economy that no type so well serves its peculiar ends as that of the gifted enthusiast whose talents verge upon genius, but in whose character are to be found defects of temperament as obvious and as fatal as those talents themselves.

For evil seeks its like, its own reflection, in its ministers. It is, indeed, its prime imperfection that it is doomed to work with tools whose temper is as unsound as its own—implements which outwardly seem trenchant and effective, but which, with the impact of use, soon lose their keenness and reveal the baseness of their alloy. The whole history of evil shows that it is capable of functioning only by fits and starts, that it does not possess the reserves and staying power of its opposite, and that, though its purpose and impulse are tireless, its vigour and judgment are unequal to the full achievement of its designs. It is proverbial that its weakest point is the pride and certainty of success which inspire it, and it is equally true that when it fails of its purpose, through the expenditure of its own vehemence, it is prone to sink back into a clownish and stupid debility.

Here one will doubtless ask for guarantees. Does a cultus of organized evil actually lurk behind the façade of Nazi Germany, and, if so, are the proofs of its existence forthcoming? Let me say at once that it is the intention of this book to bring together such proofs and to set them forth as plainly as the nature of the subject allows. It would be absurd to say that the task is not a complex one, the very nature of which makes explanation supremely difficult. Anything approaching complete success in such an undertaking is scarcely possible, but at the least a sufficiency of proof exists to enable one to remove the whole subject out of the limbo of doubt, and to make its outlines boldly apparent—so clear, indeed, that any gaps in the evidence can scarcely detract from the veracity of the general conclusions to which it points.

With the question, of course, is bound up that of organized evil as a whole, of Satanism as an ' official ' and living force. Is evil really systematized upon this planet, does it function through the operations of a central body, has it a definite locus and cult, or is it merely a thing of sporadic outbreak, working through groups which have a separate origin and which have no association one with the other ? Of some of the activities of evil it may be said, especially of the traffic in illegal drugs and the even more hideous trade in the souls of women, its normally routine activities, that the assembled representatives of the world's peoples were at no loss to assert their belief in its well-organized efforts when they set up a separate department of the League of Nations for the uprooting of these abominations.

The purpose of this mysterious and malign power has so long been recognized, and mass comprehension of it is so instinctive, that it scarcely requires definition. It is nothing less than the destruction of human civilization and the reduction of society to a condition of chaos. That, indeed, has been the Luciferian ideal throughout the ages, and those who have studied its manifestations remain in no doubt concerning their character and consequences. One is, of course, quite prepared for the chorus of dissent which will assuredly greet such a statement. There are people who still deride the affirmations of trusted students of folk-lore that witches and witchcraft continue to exist and flourish in England and the United States of America, although the clearest proofs of that existence are provided (1) and who refuse to believe that the Nazi Government has definitely sponsored an official religion of state paganism in Germany.

Unless there had been a continuous tradition of evil, a steadily cumulative growth of its powers and a definite and official leadership to put them into practice, it could never have seized its opportunities so skilfully or appropriately, or have capitalized them so successfully. But if the results of its machinations are so obvious, why is the source whence they emanate so tantalizingly obscure? The answer is that it is unveiled on occasion, as at the time of the French Revolution and at the outbreak of the Great War in 1914, but that, for the best of all reasons, its ministers take the most extraordinary pains to conceal their political and 'religious' identities by assuming the guise and character of very ordinary folk, as will become evident from what follows in subsequent chapters.

What, then, is this cult of Satanism, which, it is asserted, tirelessly functions for the undoing of humanity? Is it composed of a body of people who receive a mandate for the wreaking of general woe from the hands of the Fallen Angel in person? It has actually been claimed that certain Satanic lodges have taken their charter and received their code from Lucifer himself. (2.) But it is by no means essential for our thesis to conjure up apparitions of the Father of Evil descending upon startled councils clad in faultless evening attire. The deities of the great religions do not manifest themselves to their worshippers, even the quite mythical godlings of the lesser races are not known to appear to their suppliants. Why, then, should it be expected that the Spirit of Evil should do as much? Why should it be believed that his cultus is merely an imaginary one because he remains invisible to his servants?

Satanism is the worship of evil, the performance of its traditional behests, just as Christianity is the worship of God and the accomplishment of His law. Its ministers require no more proof of the existence of the spirit which inspires it than the Hindu does of the existence of Vishnu. In this introductory sketch of the question before us I must leave for later discussion the fuller consideration of the code and philosophy of evil and the proofs of its actual existence as the manifestation of discarnate intelligence. Just as the beneficent force enlists every opportunity for the exercise of its righteous powers, so does that of evil seize the appropriate hour to produce those results by which it hopes to alienate mankind from good and ultimately destroy it.

For centuries no such opportunity has been offered it to bring about its most cherished design as that presented by the rise and success of the Nazi Party in Germany. Nazism was not initiated by Satanism, but annexed by it. The process is as old as history. But history cannot remember a period nor a condition so appropriate to or so promising for the achievement of the grand Satanic purpose as those which have presented themselves in Germany between the years 1920 and 1940. These conditions arose out of the revengeful and jealous passions of a defeated people resolved upon the justification of its national pride and the punishment of those whom it believed to have insulted and degraded that pride by the provisions of the Treaty of Versailles. The insanity induced by its defeat in a nation which had believed itself invincible laid Germany peculiarly open to the assaults and suggestions of the Satanist caucus. It is by an examination of what has happened in Germany during these years that we may reasonably hope for a better understanding of the Luciferian power, its methods and philosophy, and even for certain data concerning its nucleus and the personnel of its administrative circles.

If something profoundly evil does not lurk behind Germany's present tyranny, where, indeed, is evil to be found ? Hitler's intent and purpose, and the foul fruits thereof, are too well known to need recapitulation. That pride, which is the basis of the Satanic heresy, is pre-eminently developed in the Nazi creed, along with its concordant vices of mendacity, subtle and cowardly distortion of the truth, assassination open and secret, the massacre and persecution of the helpless—in a word, unbridled diabolic licence. Even if it could not be proved that the Satanic power now reigns through its surrogates in Germany, that rule might justly be described, without recourse to metaphor, as Satanic. If the Prince of Darkness in person had under-

B

taken to govern that nation it is difficult to suggest how he could have borne himself otherwise than its unhappy leader has done, or with more fantastic wickedness. It is perfectly true that Hitler has done much for Germany in the merely material sense, but he has performed this task in the spirit of an inverted Jesuitism, doing good that evil might come, and as the apostle of a power which at first ever holds out great and splendid promises, only to betray its victims in the end. Of all nations Germany is the most prone to the acceptance of that evil which is tricked out in the garments of good. It is the everlasting Faust among the world's peoples, bartering its immortal spirit for the immediate glittering prize.

That Germany is chiefly animated by a desire to crush and destroy Great Britain is perhaps one of the clearest proofs of her definite alliance with the powers of evil. She professes to find in Britannia an irritating monitress who not only indulges in untimely diatribes against her methods of brigandage, but who actively interferes in a Europe the affairs of which her insular position gives her no right to participate in. In a word, the attitude of Germany to Britain is that of the criminal to the policeman—' If you were not there, what a famous time we could have.' Yet underneath this surface explanation of her dislike for this country there pulsates a deeper vein of venomous hate— the antipathy of that which is essentially slavish and darkly inspired for what is wholesome and animated by ideals of freedom and goodwill.

I cannot recall that the mystical records of nations have ever been invoked as revealing their true spiritual natures. Still, if anything is capable of throwing light upon the soul of a nation, it is surely that species of tradition which deals allegorically and mystically with its past. From this point of view, what might be called the Golden Age of British tradition, its Arthurian heyday, compares with the barbarous narrative of German myth as does the full light of chivalry with the shadows of savage craft and duplicity. The Arthurian epic is victoriously the noblest allegory of the defeat of the elements of evil by the Sons of Light ever given to the world. The chronicle of it in a hundred shapes

of stately prose and vivid poetry has done perhaps more
to inspire in our nation the love of chivalry and fair play,
and the knightly sentiment of reverence for virtue and
for womankind than any influence known to literature.
Not only so, by its appeal of sacred beauty it has urged
numberless mystics to seek the glory of the Grail, its
supreme and most lofty spiritual experience.

Compared with it, the epos of Germany, as found in the
Niebelungenlied and the *Volsunga Saga*, is an ebullition of
savagery unmitigated, in which treachery, base homicide,
and ruthless violence are the ascendent themes. And it is
over this abyss of bardic infamy that the girders which
support the columns of the temple of German hero-worship
have been thrown. Is it yet appreciated how potent are
the early traditions of a people to shape its later spiritual
attitudes and conceptions? If a nation be found ill-
balanced in its folk-philosophy one is justified in seeking
for the cause of its mal-adjustment in its myth and legendary
history.

Without hypocrisy or pharisaism it may truly and forthrightly be said that this island of Britain, despite the faults
and errors which have marred its history, and from which
no nation is exempt, has given to the world its noblest
example of a disinterested love of freedom and of the
manly virtues of courage and honest dealing, whereas the
history of Germany reveals the very reverse of these.
Here I feel compelled to say as much as having a bearing
on the proofs which must be adduced later on of the
manner in which Germany has bartered away her immortal
soul. But what, in the first instance, laid her open to the
acceptance of a bargain so fatal if it was not the tradition
of a body of legend and folk-memory which emphasized
and even glorified the qualities of revenge, jealousy, and
sanguinary violence, and which sowed the seeds of a hound-
like and sycophantic worship of that type of hero-figure
who surpasses in brute strength and dominating intimida-
tion? It was the glory of the Arthurian Round Table to
free the serf, to ameliorate the distress of the maiden
wronged, to root out violence and low cunning, whereas
the theme of the Lay of the Volsungs is the tightening of

the thrall's collar and the conquest of woman as the natural prey of the warrior. In the tales of Arthur, the magician is a wise man, grave and reverend, the minister of the tradition of a holy quest. In the German lays he is a wizard, evil and malign, the agent of powers unfriendly to humanity.

From the first Germany has been a region favourable to the suggestions of the powers of evil. Her ancient paganism, her later peasant-lore and legend, are forests of darkness almost unrelieved, her medieval magic and sorcery contain gloomier associations of diabolism than those of any other European country. In her provinces witchcraft assumed its weirdest and most abhorrent shapes. Among the many secret and arcane societies to which she gave birth between the thirteenth and sixteenth centuries, only a few can be classed as of beneficent character. Germany, it must be remembered, was the last among European communities to be converted to the Christian Faith, and even when her more central regions were nominally Christian, large tracts of the remoter dependencies were still frankly pagan. Prussia, which can scarcely be called Germany, was still in great part a heathen land in the middle of the thirteenth century, at a period when Britain had enjoyed nearly eight hundred years of Christian enlightenment.

In no country has a gloomy and haunted past cast so many shadows on the pages of its modern literature as in Germany. As we shall see, the several secret societies of evil propensity which vexed German life throughout the medieval period, such as the Vehmgerichte, were not only mischievous in their inception, but tyrannical and retrograde in their policy. With the rise of the Illuminati in the eighteenth century, the full tide of hidden treachery is attained, and Weishaupt vies with his contemporary, Frederick the Great, in Machiavellian intention and practice.

Up to this point, as I hope to prove, the links of development between the several stages of the occultism of the lower cultus in Germany are clear enough. That the Illuminist fraternity survived until 1814, if not later, one does not now require to prove, as official reports on its

activities have been discovered. It is equally clear that
from the remnant of it the Tugenbund was formed. From
that period to the rise of modern pan-Germanism with its
numerous secret and semi-secret societies, is but a short
step, and at the present time, with the data at our command, it is all but competent to say that the tradition of
an evilly inspired cultus in Germany has been active in
that country since the beginning of historic times.

But of the justice of that view the reader will have an
opportunity to form an unbiased opinion after perusing
the chapters which follow. Even those who would deny
the existence of a continuous chain of malign occult tradition in Germany would find it difficult to refuse credit to
the theory of the recurring appearance in that country of
Satanic activities which remained in abeyance for perhaps
a generation at a time, breaking out with renewed violence
from one decade to another, in the opportunist manner
characteristic of the Luciferian policy.

As regards its latter-day manifestation, the new pagan
movement in Germany, the uncompromisingly Satanic
origin of its method and intention admits of but little
dispute. The replacement of the Cross by the swastika,
the abrogation of the Sacrament in favour of a rite resembling that of the mysteries of Demeter, the persecution of
the Christian Churches and of their priests and ministers,
and the replacement of the ritual, or service, and hymn-
ology by blasphemous offices and songs, the erection of a
new godhead, the instruction of the young in the myths
of the past instead of in the Scriptures—all this affords the
clearest proof of Germany's relapse into that type of
paganism which the Satanist policy and propaganda have
invariably regarded as the most fitting medium for the
destruction and extirpation of the Christian Faith.

CHAPTER II

THE SATANIC POWER

THAT a vast and potent force for evil is once more
manifesting itself in the world and that it has seized
upon present conditions in Germany as presenting it with

a hitherto almost unrivalled opportunity for carrying into practice its designs for the destruction of mankind, is well illustrated by the declarations of those in high places who, through experience and intimate knowledge of the tides and currents of human affairs, are most competent to speak of its dire effects, both past and present. That gracious lady, the Queen of Holland, whom the Crown and people of Great Britain have gladly welcomed as an honoured guest in the hour of her country's affliction, is in no doubt of the true cause and character of the conflict which has temporarily cast the brave people of the Netherlands into the toils of a dreadful servitude.

"This," she declared in a broadcast message to the Dutch people, given on Sunday, 28 July last, "is a war between God and conscience and the powers of darkness." Indeed, that simple but eloquent statement is the verbal concentration of a sentiment already shaping itself in the minds of millions of men and women in every country in the world.

Equally striking and forceful are the terms in which Cardinal H. E. Hinsley, Archbishop of the Roman Catholic Archdiocese of Westminster, bore witness of a similar character, when, in a broadcast message to the British forces, given on 5 August last, he said : " I look upon you as champions fighting in a good cause. You are on the side of the angels in the struggle against the pride of rebellious Lucifer.   This is no exaggeration when we remember the Nazi creed of all-conquering racialism. . . . You are resisting the onslaught of brutal violence directed against the Christian values on which European civilization was founded."

Nor are the views of Dr. W. G. Whittingham, the Anglican Bishop of St. Edmundsbury and Ipswich, any less trenchant on this subject. ' We are not fighting flesh and blood,' he writes, ' but the devil, in the persons of Hitler and his gang—a gang without humanity, without pity, without right, without good, without love.'

These are only a few of the more outstanding testimonies to a belief in responsible and authoritative quarters that the malign power which has so frequently disturbed and

terrorized humanity in the past has once again roused itself
to the task of general destruction and confusion, and it is
clear that they are not couched in what is merely allegorical
language, but refer to what the speakers believe to be a
cardinal truth.

As I have said, no ruler or statesman of experience dis-
credits the existence of such a power, though some might
be hard put to it to define its actual nature and the manner
in which it functions, were they closely questioned thereon.
The general public is still more in doubt and mental confusion concerning this dark sovereignty, and not a little
dubious of its very existence. What is this Satanist or
Luciferian body which, successive writers have asserted, is
responsible for so much sorrow and unrest in human affairs?
What are its tenets, what god does it worship, who are its
agents on earth?

In the course of the next few pages I hope to provide
sufficient proofs of the existence of a Satanist power and a
Satanist Church from early times in Europe to the present
day, the members of which worshipped, and still adore,
the Father of Evil himself in his form of Lucifer, the fallen
archangel, as the spiritual symbol of rebellion, celebrating
his rites in chapels specially equipped for the purpose, most
of which have been located. This cult is the 'religious'
expression of that spirit of revolt which politically inspires
its adherents, whose main object is to carry out the command of their master to destroy a world which was the
creation of that supreme deity whom they abhor, or, alter-
natively, to do their utmost to render human life upon this
planet a chaos, and to make human progress impossible.

Now it is because the existence of such a body as I
describe appears incredible to most people of British or
American origin, that so little attention is paid in this
island and in the United States to the rumours of its
activities. It is difficult for the Anglo-Saxon to conceive
of minds so debased and so savagely inimical to human
society as to desire its destruction. It is even more difficult
for him to credit that men and women exist who actually
believe themselves to be in touch with Satan and who
strive with all their powers to carry out his doctrines with

a zeal equal to that of the most ardent Christian for his own mission.

It is just this kind of deliberate nescience and wilful blindness that makes one despair of his countrymen's political judgment. Inquire of any educated Frenchman, German, Austrian, Spaniard, or Italian if he knows of and credits the popular rumours one so frequently hears of the existence of an extensive Satanist cultus and conspiracy in Europe, and he will almost certainly at once respond in the affirmative. Of course he has heard of it, and he will probably add to your stock of knowledge concerning it. To him it is almost a topic of every day, and he will regale you with incidents of desecrated churches, stolen wafers, and the like, which have occurred in his own neighbourhood.

The comparatively comfortable standards of life in this country and the contentment which follows upon prosperity make it difficult for us to comprehend the depths of despair and envy to which thousands of people on the Continent are driven either through lack of adequate means or because of evil fortune in their personal affairs. The average European, as apart from the Briton, does not face ruin or misfortune stoically, nor does his training permit him to do so. Monetary difficulties, tragedies of the heart, the loss of position, are, it is revealed by statistics, responsible for thousands of cases of lunacy or partial alienation every year on the Continent and in proportions totally unknown in this country.

In circumstances of the kind, self-dedication to Satan is far from uncommon. The disgruntled, the disappointed the ruined, the rejected, abandon themselves to evil courses and malign devotions the mere thought of which the British man or woman would sweep aside as preposterous. In the great cities of Europe men are everywhere to be found who are known to have abjured their Christian faith in the hour of misfortune, and who are more or less regarded as outcasts.

These, of course, are merely the small fry of the congregation of Lucifer, who have been prompted to join his company in an evil moment by his active and tireless servants. In any case they are negligible, save as regards their numbers. It is those behind them who count, those powerful leaders 'who in all ages have remained concealed in remote alcoves and secret lurking-places' who are really important. These, the Grand Masters of the Cult, the instigators of world-discord, have ever succeeded in veiling themselves from the public gaze, finding perhaps, their most successful disguise in the full publicity of everyday life. Only the breeze of accident at times blows aside a corner of the mask worn by the Master Satanist, revealing the personality beneath. But such accidents are extraordinarily rare. One does not think of these, the leaders as being recruited from the unfortunate, the ruined, the defeated, but rather as the triumphantly demoniac, men who do, and worship, evil because of the perverted satisfaction they derive from its performance.

As a people we are sceptical of the existence of such devotees of evil, of human beings so peculiarly constituted that they revel in the *macabre* and the debased for its own sake, nay, exult in it, regarding it as the greatest good. We think that men and women of the kind are to be encountered merely in the pages of 'thrillers,' or the less probable kind of film. How little we know our Europe most of us ! Too often do we judge it by our own standards, forgetting that the same psychological yard-stick can never apply to all.

For there is a type of man in Continental Europe whose like is happily entirely absent from this island—whom, indeed, our insular economy could scarcely produce. He is difficult to describe, just because he is so alien to our general ideas of humanity and decency. To picture him in his entirety would make this, or any, book unsaleable. In short, to make him generally comprehensible, I cannot do better than fall back upon the time-honoured phrase of the Victorian novelette, and at once write him down as 'a fiend in human shape.'

Now this may at first sight appear as merely laughable, and I fully admit that in a certain way it is. When a type appears as comic or amusing, it has been said, it is on the way to social extinction, like the stagey old actor or the music-hall 'masher.' The mere notion of a poker-faced

B*

Luciferian nabob of the Bulwer-Lytton type, theatrical of mien, cloaked and masked, and believing himself to be the instrument of the Satanic purpose, is enough to raise a healthy British guffaw. But is he necessarily of a type so obvious ? And is it not the case that many of the notabilities who have done the world most scaith were men of appearance and manners so eccentric as to awake it to the loudest laughter in the intervals of the groans they have wrung from it ?

At the same time, care is essential in winnowing the false from the true. In the gathering of trustworthy data concerning Satanist schools in Europe we must be on our guard against the professional rumour-monger and the sensationalist. Thus, when I read, as I did lately, that in nearly every great city in this island a Satanist clique is to be found, I felt bound to deny it as a general statement and to regard it as based upon an almost fanatical nervousness and credulity. For example, I happen to reside in Edinburgh, one of the centres alluded to in this statement as harbouring a band of Luciferians. It is certainly the case that the capital of Scotland contains perhaps a higher average of mystical and occult societies than any city of its size in the United Kingdom. But, judging from the general character of its population and the membership of its occult brotherhoods, I am absolutely convinced that no such diabolist association could possibly harbour in the capital of Presbyterian Caledonia at the present time. The bare idea is grotesque, for the simple reason that Edinburgh is not a cosmopolitan community, any more than are Liverpool, Birmingham, and some of the other towns libelled in the statement alluded to, and because the native curiosity of the place, one of the keenest in Britain, would certainly prove fatal to the anonymity of such a fraternity. Some thirty years ago a charge of the kind was privately brought against a certain well-known resident, and on examining it faithfully I found it to be as baseless as it was absurd.

Indeed, I would gravely question the existence of any diabolist body in Britain outside of London, and even as regards the metropolis itself would hesitate to believe in the presence of Satanist circles other than of alien or mimetic origin, the creation of weak-minded 'amateurs' hungry for notoriety. Let us also beware of the oft-repeated suggestion that quite reputable bodies in Great Britain, cultivating one or other aspect of arcane or mystical belief, are either subject to the attentions of the Satanist cultus, or that they deliberately invite the same. The assertion has frequently been made by writers with a marked political bias, propagandists who seek everywhere to brand the most innocent, and sometimes even the most fatuous of occult, or pseudo-occult, societies as the breeding-grounds of desperately inspired anti-social movements. These assertions, indeed, do more harm to the good and righteous cause they wish to serve than their authors can well be aware of. Of course, it is by no means improbable that Satanist propagandists may seek to sow the seeds of their cult in one or other of these societies, but that they have prevailed to any extent, any more than in the case of the Churches, where they possibly also carry on their work of infidelity, is much too improbable an idea to entertain.

Let us now turn to the question of the development of the Satanist power in Europe in as critical and scientific a frame of mind as possible. By so doing, indeed, we shall gather sufficient proof of its existence without accepting the wild assertions of those whose chief intention is either to bias us politically or to make our flesh creep.

The question of the origin of good and evil may be posed either theologically or considered from a philosophical viewpoint. The first is associated with what is known to students of Comparative Religion as 'dualism,' that is the view which seeks to explain the scheme of things by alleging the existence of two independent and absolute spiritual elements, a good and an evil. Such an opposition of light and darkness has been found as a cardinal principle in the religious history of many races in all parts of the world—in ancient Egypt, where Osiris and Set were opposed to one another; in old Babylon, where Merodach and Tiawath strove for supremacy; among the ancient Persians, whose god of light, Ormuzd, ceaselessly combated the dark Ahriman; in classical Greece, where Zeus and Typhon were ranged one against the other; and in Scandinavia, the opponents being Thor, the Thunder-god, and Loki, the cunning and knavish spirit of mischief. Many barbarous races to-day also reveal this quality of dualism in their religions, for example, more than one of the North American Indian tribes, the Australian Black-fellows, the Hottentots, and the Banks Islanders. (3.)

It is a fact in Folklore that the most primitive races have no sense of right and wrong, and that the gods or spirits they worship are not regarded as having the quali-ties of good and evil. The sense of sin and wrong-doing is associated only with a higher phase of religious belief, when 'conscience' has been awakened by long experience of the danger of breaking taboos, or social rules, sacred, tribal, or personal. The idea of sin becomes 'spiritualized,' so to speak. It takes on a definite personal shape, that of an evil entity, with whom everything that is unfortunate and disastrous is associated.

Such, stated very briefly, is the anthropological view of the problem. The theological or philosophical attitude to it is somewhat more complex. The latest deliverance from this source is that of Dr. Richard Króner, Emeritus Pro-fessor of Kiel University, as set forth in his Gifford Lectures, delivered at St. Andrews University in November, 1939. Evil, says Dr. Króner, has no natural quality, but is known to man only because he is a willing and acting being. Evil is a quality of the will alone, though not a natural quality of it, as, for example, sweetness belongs to sugar. It is rather a quality which the will acquires in the act of willing, for it is the will which shapes itself as good or evil. Good and evil are opposite ends to which man's conduct is directed, opposite directions in which he can will by his own volition.

Good is positive because it is the principle of order and the standard of judgment in the moral order. As a rule it is one and single, while evil, as the negation of rule, is multiple, and without order and system. So that good has no opposite reality confronting it at all. It stands beyond all contrasts, because evil is not a principle equal and opposite to the principle of good. It is merely the denial of principle altogether, an out-and-out negation.

To my way of thinking, this does not sufficiently account
for the active principle in evil, that which inspires men to
deeds of violence and wickedness, and which is certainly
not a negative quantity. Nor would it appear to square
with the belief of Dean Inge, who has said : " I have not
the slightest doubt that Christians are enjoined to believe
in a positive malignant spiritual power." By far the
greater number of practical Christian thinkers, I believe,
would agree with this statement. Of the presence of evil
and destructive forces on this sad star of ours we cannot
be ignorant, and the question whether we create these
ourselves, to our own loss and misery, out of ' original
sin,' or whether they emanate from entities ever on the
watch to harm and afflict us, has for ages presented an
argument profoundly disquieting.

But here common experience triumphs over philosophical abstraction. The whole history of human progress,
civilization, in the true sense of the term, has been of a
struggle to escape from the bonds of ignorance and all
the vileness accruing to a lower and merely animal condition. During this struggle the prime aspects of good and
evil have become sufficiently concrete and well-defined to
permit of classification as absolute qualities and not mere
freakish accidents of thought, time, and geography. If we
are to admit the existence of the spiritual at all, we cannot
dissociate either of these opposing qualities from the idea
of spirit.

The Christian idea of a power of evil, a Satan, was
developed from early Jewish belief, as, in the Book of
Job, for example, where he plays the part of tempter or
seducer. This aspect of him, in turn, was almost certainly
developed from the idea of the serpent of Genesis, the evil
spirit which brought about the fall of our first parents,
and which is a figure of some importance in the Rabbinical
writings of Jewry. At a later stage, when the idea of
dualism had become more familiar to the Jewish theologians, we behold a more definitely personalized Satanic
presence in Beelzebub, prince of all the evil spirits.

But Christianity seems to have accepted as its earliest
dualistic figure that Lucifer who was first alluded to by

Isaiah as 'the Morning Star,' the rebel against divine authority. This is, however, not the title given to the evil principle in the Apocalypse of St. John, who, in his account of the battle in heaven between the Archangel Michael and the rebel angels, alludes to their chief as 'the dragon,' 'the devil,' and 'Satan,' who was 'cast down unto the earth and his angels were thrown down with him.' The cause of offending of this rebellious spirit is nowhere specifically mentioned, but there is a general concensus of opinion that its roots were to be found in that Satanic pride which has become proverbial in association with the legend of his fall, a pride which was ambitious of equality, at the least, with his Maker, and which could brook neither discipline nor the thought of loyalty.

In some quarters an impression seems to prevail that diabolism was the mere invention of the early Christian Church, a species of bogey contrived by it to keep the masses in terrified subjection. As the Church did its utmost not only to extirpate diabolism, but even to destroy its very name, the charge is as illogical as it is unfounded. Diabolism, in much the same form as it was known to the early Christian missionaries, had, indeed, been the uncompromising foe of the official religion of imperial Rome long before the advent of Christianity. In pre-Christian times Tiberius was compelled to exile all practitioners of black magic from Rome, passing sentence of death upon the most notorious, while Claudius, Vitellius, and Vespasian meted out to them an equal severity.

When at last Christianity was accepted as the official religion of Rome, by the decree of the Emperor Constantine in the year A.D. 324, it became, almost at once, the natural target for the assaults of diabolism and its adherents. By this time the diabolic tradition had been enormously reinforced by the beliefs and practices introduced into Europe by Eastern fraternities and sects which more or less openly practised the worship of evil. One of the most outstanding of these was the Manichæan heresy, a sect which had its rise in Asia Minor under a half-legendary Mani, and which combined the remnants of the superstitions of Gnosticism and Zoroastrianism with some of the principles of Christianity. (4.) One of its chief doctrines was that of dualism, and a lopsided dualism at that, for it believed that all matter is evil in its origin, and that even humanity was of Satanic origin.

Wave after wave of Manichæism rolled across Europe. In A.D. 556 a number of its immigrant apostles were executed at Ravenna. But about the year 1000, when many Christians believed the world was about to come to an end, Manichæism received a considerable accession to its numbers, and a new era of popularity began for it. By the year 1200 it had spread across southern Europe and had reached Germany. Later, it split up into a bewildering number of minor sects, such as the Bogomiles, the Aldonistæ, the Cathari, and a host of other minor bodies. The Bogomiles openly worshipped Satan and rejected all the Christian sacraments. Under the name of Cathari they spread into southern France, Italy, and Germany, impressing their dreadful doctrines upon the people wherever they went.

The ideas underlying the Bogomile cult are important as indicating a very definite link with later Satanism. (5.) Christ and Satanael, they claimed, were both the sons of God, but Satanael, the elder, rebelled against his Father, and was thrust out of Heaven. With the assistance of his numerous followers he created the material world and man. In order to defeat his purpose, Christ came to earth, but failed to succeed in His mission of enlightenment and saving grace. Satanael had, therefore, been triumphant, and was obviously the true God. Because of this doctrine the Bogomiles came to be known, first as 'Satanists' and later as 'Luciferians,' according to their belief that Lucifer, or Satanael, would one day be restored as the Lord of Heaven. In the latter part of the twelfth century Luciferianism, or the later phase of the Bogomile doctrine, had spread from the Balkan Peninsula, its earliest European home, to the Tyrol, Bohemia, and Germany, and a couple of centuries afterwards had established itself in France and Italy. By this time it had cast aside its earlier pretensions to dualism and now boldly announced its adherence to the doctrine of evil for evil's sake.

The spread of these doctrines, all of them bearing a strong basic resemblance to each other, and mainly of Eastern origin, was greatly assisted by the accession of beliefs and superstitions from the ancient diablerie of Europe itself, native to the soil, the detritus of the broken-down religions which had been thrust into outer darkness by the official acceptance of Christianity, but thousands of whose devotees still clung to them, carrying on a species of subterranean warfare against the Christian faith. Even kings, on occasion, gave countenance to these heresies. Philip of France, who reigned for forty-eight years, from 1060 to 1108, appears to have done his utmost to quash sentences passed against heretics in the ecclesiastical courts and to have banished and persecuted the bishops who had sat in judgment upon them.

The black sorcery of the Middle Ages was thus the fruit of heresy which had mingled with the native superstitions of Europe, derived from the remains of pagan religions superseded by Christianity. Witchcraft was, perhaps, the most outstanding and popular example of that admixture, and in its essence was one with the worship of Lucifer, especially in its later expression, when it appears to have developed into a mere Satanist cultus. There were, however, elements in 'official' Luciferianism which revealed a more elaborate and mystical ritual and dogma, thus showing that it was a rather more advanced type of the popular diabolic system of witchcraft suited to the notions of a more cultivated and subtle taste and following. Persons of loftier rank practised Luciferianism in the early centuries as the lower orders practised witchcraft, and chapels and dedicated chambers took the place of the deserted heath or the remote hill-side, the *al fresco* temples of the Great Enemy.

Still, there was a difference. The old religions, those native to the soil, had not in their prime existed for the purpose of doing evil for evil's sake. So far as it was given to their ministers, they were, if not actually beneficent, at least not evil, but merely 'amoral,' or nearly so, founded as they were on the idea of a primitive bargain, with the gods for material aid. Witchcraft and Satanism, on the other hand, existed for no other purpose than the commission of evil at the behest of the dark master who dictated their abominations.

As the Dark Ages merged into the Middle Ages, Satanism, from a heresy, grew into a definite cult, with no fixed centre, but with widespread ramifications in Europe. It is alleged by some authorities that the charge against the Knights Templar that they worshipped the Fiend in the likeness of a goat or a hideous four-faced god, the Baphomet, is founded on fact, but of this no trustworthy proof appears to be forthcoming. One of the earliest medieval cases of the goetic worship in France is that of Lucas de Lafond, a priest of the see of Toulouse, whose mistress publicly accused him of celebrating the black mass. In 1340 he was sentenced to imprisonment for life. A century later we have the truly atrocious *cause célèbre* of Gilles de Rais, the French ' Bluebeard,' whose abominations are much too well known to need rehearsal. Enough to say that Gilles was a thoroughgoing Satanist as well as a sadist and black magician. (6.)

In the year 1588—to give something approaching chronological sequence to this pageant of horrors—Henry III, King of France, son of the terrible Catherine de Medici, was assassinated, and there seem to be grounds for the assumption that his death had been privately inflicted because of his Satanist leanings. It was said that a grove in the forest of Vincennes was the scene of the diabolist worship of this miserable degenerate, and that he adored two silver images of satyrs which were later discovered there, along with a golden cross and the remains of a slaughtered child. Other and even more dreadful tales recounted of this royal cretin scarcely bear repetition.

The case of Louis Gaufridi, a priest of Marseilles, is also among the most celebrated in these infamous annals. In the year 1611 the convent of the Order of Ursulines at Aix was thrown into confusion by the convulsionary attacks of several of the nuns who resided there ; one of whom, Sister Madeleine, charged Gaufridi with having brought about her possession by devils. Gaufridi was arrested, and at his trial Madeleine fully confessed her share in the abominable rites they had celebrated along with others. Gaufridi was compelled to confess his fiendish iniquities, and was burned at the stake. (7.) The well-known case of the priest Urbain Grandier and the nuns of Loudun is rather one of witchcraft and diabolic possession than of Satanism, and no Luciferian rites appear to have been celebrated by this apostate cleric, who was burnt for his abominable crimes in 1634, although it is noticeable that the practice of black magic is included in the indictment against him.

Even more dreadful, perhaps, were the ghastly horrors associated with the trial of Madeleine Bavent, a Franciscan nun of Louviers, who in 1647 confessed that she and three chaplains of the convent had revived the heresy of the Adamites, a Gnostic sect, who celebrated the black mass in a state of nature. The foul rites with which this monstrous quartetté defiled things sacred led to the burning of one of the chaplains—the sole survivor of the three priests impeached—while Madeleine, who appears to have been the witless instrument of these lost wretches, was immured in a dungeon for life. (8.)

A frightful orgy of Satanic sacrilege broke over Paris in the reign of Louis XIV, which seems to have been an organized, if subterranean, revolt against religion. The black mass was celebrated in hundreds of private houses and licence ran wild. The head and front of this movement appears to have been the Abbé Guiborg—strange how priests were so frequently implicated !—of whom it might well have been written, as Byron did of ' Monk ' Lewis :

> 'E'en Satan's self might fear with thee to dwell.
> And in thy skull discern a deeper hell.'

This wretch, a brutal and overbearing monster of callousness, and his associates, mainly Churchmen of some standing, were regular celebrants of the black mass, and by the aid of La Voisin, a *femme sage* of Paris, and a notorious poisoner and procureuse, they gathered together such an infernal company of bohemians, players, wanton aristocrats and nameless creatures from the stews and slums of Paris as to make up a devil's carnival probably unrivalled in the history of Satanism. A vile traffic in drugs was also carried on by these miscreants and even Madame de Montespan, the King's favourite, and scores of the nobility, were dragged into the demoniac circle, the impious and sacrilegious rage of which seems to have known no bounds.

The chief centre of the horrible rites celebrated by Guiborg and the more ' select ' of his desperate crew was a private chapel near Montlhery, where, in the fantastic robes of a magical practitioner, this devil-ridden wretch carried out his abominable rites upon a pretended human 'victim,' stretched naked upon the altar. There seem, however, to have been many real sacrifices of unfortunate infants, whose bodies were afterwards burnt. Later, it was proved beyond doubt that a regular traffic in very young children had been carried on by La Voisin, who procured subjects for this holocaust from women of ill-repute who had borne them in secret.

A scandal of such immense proportions naturally followed, in which persons of the highest eminence were involved, that the King was compelled to put a sudden period to the police proceedings, but not until European society at large had been horror-struck and nauseated by the appalling rumours concerning the affair. This case may be regarded as marking one of the heydays of the Satanist cult and as revealing its wide ramifications among, and deadly effects upon, civilized European society. (9.)

From that time onward the record revealing the continuity of Satanism in France is sufficiently plain. The Duc de Richelieu, the Regent Philippe d'Orleans and the atrocious Marquis de Sade were certainly among the professors of devil-worship in a France grown rotten and decadent, and more prone to abomination than any other European country of that age. Still, in Germany, Italy, and other lands the horror had not ceased to manifest itself sporadically, and the French Revolution, as we shall see, gave it still further impetus.

Coming down to more modern times, we have on record a well-documented series of examples of Satanic practice. So dreadful had the scourge become in 1803 that the Abbé Fiard believed the coming of Antichrist to be at hand. At

Agen, in Guyenne, anciently a diabolist centre, the Luciferians appear to have been most active from 1817 to 1840, and the number of desecrations to their discredit during these years was very considerable. The case of the nun, Sister Cantianille, of the convent of Mont-Saint-Sophie at Auxerre, who had been dedicated to Satan by an apostate priest, disclosed a shocking condition of things, and it was found necessary to exorcize the demons which were said to possess her. Her confessions of demonic orgies were so unspeakably vile that she was banished from the ecclesiastical see by the Bishop in 1865.

Thirty years passed without bringing any flagrant instances of diabolism to light. In 1895, however, the veil was lifted in good earnest from the Satanist altar, and those who believed diabolism to be an invention of the sensational novelist or the journalist hard up for 'copy,' were sharply disillusioned. What was now revealed, indeed, was one of those rare instances of the definite existence of the cult—a fully equipped Satanist chapel.

The family of the Borghese in Rome had let part of their ancestral palazzo in separate flats to various lessees. After a time, their agents experienced some difficulty in gaining admission to certain apartments situated on the mezzanine floor. This they could not quite understand, as, by the terms of the rental, they had permission to inspect the mansion at stated intervals, so that they might make arrangements regarding any necessary repairs, and as the owner was about to be married and intended to occupy the palace, it was essential that matters should be hastened.

So the agents demanded the keys, which were handed to them by the tenant with the greatest reluctance, particularly as regards those of one apartment. On entering it, the astonished visitors were amazed to find it disposed and embellished as a chapel of Satan. On the walls were painted the words 'Templum Palladium,' it was hung with-black and scarlet curtains of silk, so that no light could enter, while at the extreme end was stretched a large tapestry, on which a gigantic figure of Lucifer was displayed, beneath which lay an altar provided with all the apparatus of infernal worship—black candles, grotesque vessels for use in the black mass, and unholy books. We have it on the authority of Monseigneur de Ségur that in 1848 a similar chapel was discovered in Rome, and, as we shall see, the general arrangement of these infamous dens was almost invariably the same.

Mr. Montague Summers, whose scholarly and carefully documented works on witchcraft supply so many instances of Satanic activity, furnishes us with an authentic account gleaned from the personal experiences of a Monsieur Serge Basset, a French journalist of repute, who published them in the columns of *Le Matin*, in May 1899. Monsieur Basset had written an article for *L'Eclair*, in which he took occasion to ridicule the prevailing belief in the existence of Satanism in Paris. Shortly afterwards, he received a letter which invited him to be a witness of the celebration of the black mass. He ignored it, but received a call from a heavily veiled lady, who requested him to accompany her in her car to the scene of the infernal celebration.

Arriving at the rendezvous, a large house in a lonely street, he was ushered into a chapel where some seven or eight persons, mostly women, were seated. Through the gloom of the place, which was lit by a single lamp, he beheld an altar, and when six candles were presently lit he saw, squatting upon it, a huge living goat, the veritable adored image of Luciferian tradition. The walls of the place were elaborately decorated with pentacles, stars, and other goetic symbols, interspersed with lewd pictures and designs.

The celebrant, a tall man, dressed in grotesque robes, commenced his unholy ritual, thick clouds of incense arose, and the words of the black mass were muttered in low tones. A naked girl crouched before the altar, offering herself as if for sacrifice. She mounted it, and the black host was elevated. The celebrant scattered a number of black hosts to the worshippers, who rushed upon the altar with fanatical frenzy, tearing off their clothes as they did so. This proved too much for Monsieur Basset, who placed his hands over his eyes with an exclamation of disgust. Two men, who had been observing him, at once rushed upon him and hurried him from the chamber. Upon the publication of his article doubts were cast on its authenticity, but he pledged his word that what he had described was true in every detail. (10.)

In his enlightening work, *Le Pouvoir Occulte Contre la France*, Monsieur Copin Albancelli has made it clear that certain debased Masonic societies in France at that time (1908) were indulging in Satanic practices. He alleged their adoration of Lucifer, and claimed that their formula, expressed by capital letters, signified : 'Glory and Love to Lucifer. Hate ! hate ! hate ! to God, accursed ! accursed ! accursed !' All that the Christian God commands, he added, was hateful to this society, and to Lucifer, and all that He forbids is agreeable to the fallen angel. 'I repeat,' he writes, ' that so far as those things are concerned, I have proof ready and at hand.' (11.)

In December 1919, the *Daily Express* published a message from its Berlin correspondent which gave an account of the dispersion of a gang of devil-worshippers in the German capital. A posse of police, over a hundred strong, descended upon them in their place of orgy in the Café Kerkau and surprised some five hundred naked wretches with all the apparatus of their hideous worship about them. After a brief resistance, they were removed in large vans and it was hinted that several persons of eminence were among their number.

In 1926 a case which startled all France occurred. The Abbé Desnoyers, the parish priest of Bombon, near Melun, was seriously assaulted in his sacristy by a number of men who were arrested by the police. When his assailants, mostly persons of some consequence, were brought before the magistrates they accused the Abbé of being ' Satan ' and alleged that he had brought foul diseases upon Bordeaux, which were transmitted by birds, whose droppings caused fungi, giving off such dreadful odours that those who inhaled them were immediately smitten with sickness. The Abbé, they said, was an infamous sorcerer. The affair seems to have ended in public ridicule.

In 1931 a *fama* concerning the local practice of necromancy broke out at Helsingfors (Helsinki) in Finland and it was alleged that the influences which fomented this proceeded from a society in London known as ' The Black International.' The local newspapers stated that the

Finnish police had called in the assistance of Scotland Yard in order that the menace might be quelled at its source. I cite these last two instances as proof of the fact that certain rumours regarding Satanism are quite as absurd as some are genuine.

The above are only a few of the hundreds of such episodes which occurred at varying periods in practically every European country. So far, however, I have drawn my 'illustrations' mainly from France, chiefly because the history of Satanic worship is more consecutively apparent in that country, and is better recorded than in Germany, whose occult history I will deal with at some length in the following chapter.

Before doing so, however, it will be necessary to give some description of the black mass. The chapel is sometimes specially dedicated to the infernal powers, but, on occasion, private Christian sanctuaries and churches have been used for its celebration. The altar differs in no way from that in use in most Roman Catholic places of worship. Upon it is almost invariably placed the Sabbatic goat, either alive, as in the case observed by Monsieur Basset, or in image. The candles flanking this effigy are supposed to be black, and made of the fat of executed criminals, although this can scarcely be the case to-day.

Foul water is used for asperging, and a fetid incense, compounded of rue, henbane, deadly nightshade, resin, and rotting leaves is burned in braziers and thuribles. The host is said to contain altar-bread of a somewhat reddish hue, but is frequently a wafer stolen from a Catholic church, upon which nameless indignities are done. The host and chalice employed in this dread communion are frequently black and of curious shape. Sometimes the wafer is stamped with the devil's name and occasionally this is written upon it in characters of blood.

The mass is read from a missal specially composed, in which the usual procedure of the celebration is inverted and parodied. The vestments worn by the celebrant were sometimes black, but on occasion they appear to have been the worn-out robes of a priest or bishop, torn, stained, and shabby, though not infrequently the celebrant was orthodox in his habiliments, these including the usual chasuble, stole, maniple, and the other articles of ecclesiastical wear suitable to the occasion.

The celebration usually began with an invocation to Satan, after which the worshippers confessed any good they had done, upon which penance was inflicted. To absolve them, the inverted sign of the cross was made with the left hand. The hosts were then brought to the altar, and the chalice filled, with what is not clear, but it was said to be a nauseous liquor, bitter and harsh to the taste. At the elevation of the host, the wretches who took part in this profanation uttered the most appalling screams and wild blasphemies, while the celebrant howled his obscenities. To conclude the service, the 'blessing' given was usually an adjuration to the congregation to betake themselves with all speed to the Fiend. Occasionally the foulest sacrifices were offered up and the murder of unfortunate infants on the altar appears to have been much more general among Satanists or Luciferians than the sistercult of witchcraft.

We see, then, that so far from being a sporadic cult only occasionally celebrated by a few isolated eccentrics here and there, Satanism was, and is, a creed not only of consequence, historically speaking, but continuous in its establishment and its records and enthusiastic in its propaganda, semi-secret though that must naturally be. And that its tradition is being upheld at the present time with perhaps more infernal vigour than at any period in its long history must surely be apparent to all persons of observation and experience. May it be given to this generation to extirpate for ever its abominations and to relegate even the memory of this most malodorous passage in human affairs to that forgetfulness which is nature's prison-house for the base and the unnatural.

CHAPTER III

THE SATANIC POWER IN OLD GERMANY

NO European country holds so dark a record of ancient sorcery and horror as old Germany. Curious and grimly bizarre as are certain passages in the occult history of France, vile and subtly tortuous as is the maze of medieval Italian diabolism, naïvely terrific as are the superstitions of the Balkan lands, there resides in the spirit of ancient German black magic and folk-belief a sentiment of the weird and the hideous that remains unsurpassed in the whole chronicle of European arcana. In traversing this dread tract of German myth and legend it is as if one were passing through a seemingly endless forest where scarcely the faintest beam of daylight is able to pierce the thick and fetid glooms, and where the grotesque outlines of gnarled and twisted trunks and boles mimicked the shapes of those demonic denizens of German fables—nixes, erl-kings, and herlikini, kobolds, nornas, and alps, wild women and durs—which have ever haunted, and still haunt, the German mind. Menacing and appalling as some of the dark forms of Celtic folk-fancy certainly are—gruagachs, kelpies, and ourisks—still they have a friendly and human si to them denied to the offspring of the German imagination, as is found in the pages of Grimm, Goethe, and Sophus Bugge, those peerless masters of the mysteries of the Teutonic soul.

Indeed no region in Europe can rival Germany in the gloomy fantasy of her imagination, no more fitting culture-bed could have been devised for the growth and development of beliefs at once cruel and primitive, or so relentless in their hold upon the mind and heart of a people. With the approach of civilization and education the Celt, in the Scottish Highlands and in Ireland and Wales, even in Brittany, has cast aside the trappings of his ancient superstitions, until to-day only the faintest shadows of these remain as something to haunt the background of folk-memory rather than to dominate it. But, whatever may be said to the contrary, the German has clung with an indefeasible persistency to the timeless beliefs of his fathers, his weird soul is still wrapt about with their sorceries, escape them he cannot. Heart and spirit are inextricably trammelled by their mystic nets and bonds. Ostensibly, he may be in the forefront of progress, but the slave of a pagan idea he still remains at heart. And in the renaissance of that paganism, as expressed in his 'new' national religion, he is once more revealing his thraldom to those dark and persistent forces to an astonished world.

It is not alone his consistent conservatism which enchains him to these haunting memories of a sombre past. He is the known victim of a strange, almost dog-like fidelity to evil as well as good conventions which has restrained his mental liberties and retarded his political manumission. Witt Doehring, a German intriguer who had taken part in many of the subterranean activities of secret societies in his country, when interrogated by a legal court at Bayreuth, in 1824, gave contemptuous expression to this attribute of the German mind. He said that in his opinion the great obstacle to the spread of liberal sentiments in Germany was the servile character and ' dog-like fidelity ' of the German people, who were in the habit of giving an unreasoning and instinctive adherence to their leaders. A French correspondent of the Abbé Barruel bore similar witness to this extraordinary docility. The German people, he says, are so slavish and sheep-like that none of the influences of democracy or liberal thought can penetrate their minds. And they have remained as psychologically servile to the basic ideals of their pristine faith as to their equally ancient political attitudes.

For the grey volume of German paganism is by no means closed. For centuries it has lain open, side by side with the Scriptures. Not only was Germany the last among European countries to accept the Christian faith, but in no other land was it accepted with so ill a grace. Repeated massacres of priests by the enraged people followed upon the conversion of their kings. Gotzbert, Duke of Thuringia, was slain by his subjects because he had accepted conversion at the hands of the Celtic St. Kilian, after which the Thuringian folk adopted a strange admixture of Christianity and paganism, precisely as the more ' cultured ' Nazis of the self-same region are doing to-day. Strangely enough, indeed, it is from this very Thuringian land that many of the principles of the new ' Positive ' Christianity have come, which reveals that in more than a thousand years the German soul has not appreciably altered in its general outlook.

Paganism prevailed in an idol-ridden Prussia until the end of the tenth century. Its apostle, Adalbert, was murdered by the heathen Prussians, but his labours were carried on by Bruno, an Italian brother, whom they also butchered. So doggedly heathen-minded were the Prussians, indeed, and such outrages did they commit upon those who sought to proselytize them, that at last it was found necessary to occupy their country by a military brotherhood, the Teutonic Knights, who, proceeding from Palestine in the thirteenth century, undertook to convert or conquer those intractable and dangerous savages, who still maintained an idolatrous faith of a particularly low grade in the forests and fastnesses of Prussia and Livonia at a period when Britain, or most of it, had been Christian for more than seven hundred years.

The ancient faith of Germany and Scandinavia, popularly known as 'the religion of Odin and Thor,' has been the subject of many a literary encomium. To myself, as a student of Folklore and Mythology, it makes an appeal no more gracious or stimulating than any other religion of the lower cultus, and very much less so than those even of Polynesia or old Peru.

It is, indeed, only the fact that it is being resuscitated by extreme Nazi fanatics which makes it important at all, and, even so, it is worthy of notice only in a temporary sense, for with the downfall of Hitler and his caucus it will go the way of all artificially revived heterodoxies.

The ancient Teutonic religious system is, indeed, one of those faiths which are rather mythologies than religions. It is an agglomeration of myth and tale, which might really be labelled 'Adventures of the Gods,' rather than a well-digested system having behind it a solid background of dogma and ethical ideality. It may be objected that this holds good of most early faiths. Not so. The Celtic mind developed the profundities of Druidism, which, intensive research is now showing, had a very real existence and a sound tradition of lofty thought to commend it. Moreover, it is known that in many cases Druidic communities in Britain and Ireland regarded Christianity as the natural sequel to the later and more highly developed Druidic ideals and aspirations and accepted it with joy and thanksgiving, many Druid Officiants becoming Christian priests. The Jewish faith, a much more venerable system than the Teutonic, had a mystical side of extraordinary richness, which has had powerful repercussions upon the religious thought of humanity as a whole, and the same may be said of the great religions of old Egypt and Babylonia. These could boast of interesting and skilfully conceived mythologies, and were fortunate in the possession of ethical beliefs and canons of thought and doctrine regarding life and eternity which have not only excited the admiration of all who have studied them, but which have been accepted as the basis of much that is valuable and permanent in mystical philosophy. China and India, too, brilliant mythologically in their ancient conceptions of the gods, are none the less wonderfully inspired in theological reflection and spiritual and philosophical scope and flight.

But no such lofty or penetrating beliefs or ideals are to be discovered in the crude religious groping of 'the Blonde Beast,' as one of its chief protagonists has entitled the Germanic prototype. Among the Celtic peoples the home of the gods is that insular paradise—by no means a 'heaven' in the strict sense of the term—where the immortals dwell in an everlasting rapture of addiction to the arts of music and poesy and the consideration of the cult of beauty, that Tir-nan-Oge which has become confused with the idea of 'Fairyland.' Compared with this, the Valhalla of the Germanic tribes, with its barbarous feastings, its combats and its atmosphere of savage warrior-life, presents a scene of riotous debauchery and oafish horse-play, re-echoing with ferocious boasts and challenges.

It is from this rude and grossly martial tradition, as we shall see at a later stage, that the 'theologians' of the new German faith attempt to wrest implications and doctrines suitable to modern ethical circumstances, and labour to bring forward suggestions, framed in the uttermost agony of perverted fancy, to prove that the germs of a great system of folk-belief and natural theology, as well as a moral code, lay dormant in its violent and homicidal confusion, which, through the genius of modern research and casuistry, may be erected into a noble and 'shining' faith agreeable to the 'soldier soul' of the latter-day Nordic. But the endeavour is as hopelessly fantastic as that which would try to make the proverbial purse out of the proverbial sow's ear. And, indeed, the inventors of this monstrous parody of a cultus have of themselves divined as much, and realizing that their prentice and clumsy attempts at developing a new Germanic creed have failed utterly, have, in their perplexity, reverted to the desperate expedient of foisting upon Germanity the whole crude and chaotic mass of the pagan beliefs of its early barbaric ancestors, very much as those are to be found in the twin 'gospels' of the Elder and Younger Eddas, accompanied by such doctrinal smatterings of their own as might appear to redeem the project from the charge of plagiarism and irrationality.

This grey and loveless aggregation of barbarous lay and legend, the apotheosis of tumult and bloodshed, which inspired the bloody-minded Viking to the commission of a thousand brutal atrocities in his raids upon European civilization, is, we are told, to become the future 'religion' of the German folk, the tradition in which the hapless youth of Germany is to be led and nurtured. The homicidal fanaticism of the Viking, the sacker of Christian churches and prosperous settlements, the ruffianly despoiler of abbeys, the first among Europe's slave-traders and the Gothic destroyer of her ancient culture!

It is from the Elder Edda, discovered by the Icelandic Bishop Bryngulf Sveinsson, about 1643, and attributed to the historian Saemund, who was born towards the middle of the eleventh century, that we receive our most complete knowledge of the Teutonic belief. This collection of some five-and-thirty songs and lays is chiefly mythological in its aspect, but in many places deals also with hero-tale and primitive magical knowledge, most of which appear to date about a century before Saemund's time and to have been collected rather than inspired by him. The theory of Sophus Bugge, as given in his *Home of the Eddic Poems*, (12) that it was not a genuine body of traditional belief, but a merely fictitious compilation imitated from Christian and Jewish classical models, aroused a storm of opposition in Germany in the eighties of last century among those critics who believed that it issued out of the Viking spirit of the seventh and eighth centuries. Bugge's theory that it was composed by Norwegian poets in Britian and that it drifted thence, by way of Scotland, to Iceland, was also furiously combated.

The most important and interesting of these ancient poems is the ' Völuspà,' or prophecy of the Völva, or Sybil, who from her lofty seat addresses Odin, singing of the primeval times before even the gods were created, of the origin of the Jötunn, of men and dwarfs, and of the last dreadful doom in the 'twilight of the gods' at Ragnorök. The whole composition is intensely mysterious in both atmosphere and wording, but shows much confused knowledge of a cosmology different from that of later Scandinavian times, and is on the whole extremely difficult to understand. Next we have ' Hàvamàl ' (' Lesson of the High One '), a collection of saws and proverbs, containing a series of stories told by Odin to his own discomfiture. The cosmogony and chronology of the Scandinavian religion are set forth in the 'Vafprùthnismàl,' or ' Lesson of Vafprùthnir,' a giant who is visited by Odin in disguise and catechized by him.

Many burlesque stories of the gods are also told in ' The Journey of Skirnir,' ' The Lay of Hoarbeard,' and 'The Brewing of Ægir.' The rest of the Poetic Edda is concerned with pseudo-history, and, among other things, with the long and important series of lays relating to the two heroic families of the Volsungs and the Nivelungs. These, however, are not so much myth as hero story.

The Prose, or Younger, Edda is a miscellaneous group of writings collected by Snorri Sturlason (1178–1241), who completed the work about 1222. The name ' Edda ' does not appear to have been originally bestowed upon it by its author, and Scandinavian scholars find some difficulty in explaining it. It was, it is thought, composed by different hands between the years 1140 and 1160. It is divided into four parts, with a preface, which, after the fashion of that period, purports to furnish the reader with a history of human affairs from the beginning.   The second part, ' Gylfaginning,' or ' The Delusion of Gylfi,' is a valuable compendium of early Scandinavian myth.   The third part, the ' Bragaræ thur,' or ' Sayings of Bragi,' contains mythical poems attributed to Bragi, the god of poetry.

And what of the gods whose rugged and gigantic forms are to be glimpsed through the wrack of this drift and shadow of ancient myth ?   It is important that we should not permit a distaste for Nazi ideals to strain our judgment concerning the standards of this Nordic Olympus.   Still, I say with candour and such patience as I can bring to its consideration, that I feel supremely uneasy in its company. As a Scotsman I naturally feel at home among the Celtic gods, dreading never as much as a shade of that gloom which, a stupid modern tradition avers, is their native element (an absurd piece of Anglo-Irish invention, put about by the stagey and precious poets of Dublin) and even half a century of rubbing shoulders with the bogey-like deities of old Mexico has aroused in me no more distaste of them than a detective-inspector at Scotland Yard might feel for the ' big shots ' of crime.

But for those whey-faced butchers of the viks and their gods I confess I have no stomach.   The whole burden of their song—a canticle of abundant flatness, long-drawn to the verge of exhaustion—is one of blood, and then more blood except where it changes its key and keens of the raptures of loot and rapine, of the gold rings taken on the field of swords from dead fingers, of the whirling of raven-women in the lift over the moor of the broken bynies, of the incineration of ship and body, when some chieftain of more than usually homicidal temperament, who had at last met his match, drove out to sea, with flame for his canvas and sparks for his pennant.

And that is really all—a raucous rant of redness, a grey arras splashed with gore, athwart which vast and grotesque shadows hurtle and wrangle—save, perhaps, that one hears the echoes of the chucklings of knavery, the rascal cachinnations of the weak but subtle, who, unable to front those elephantine gods in combat, devised nets and springs for them, and at last brought them to their twilight and their end.

This is the mythology of the 'killer,' and to attempt to construe it as in any sense symptomatic or incipient, in its gross and furious naïvety, of ideals more exalted, to read into it, as do its Nazi apologists, the possibilities of development into a faith conformable to the mental attitudes of civilization is not only to write oneself down an ass, but as devil's advocate, which is very much the same thing. It is, it always has been, in such brutal and primitive reflections of the barbaric mind that the force we call Satan or Lucifer finds the choicest generative bed for the red seed he sows. Scarcely a word of even rude wisdom accompanies these sanguinary scufflings and knavish stratagems as moral commentary. Even the cosmological side of the system, which tells of the creation of the world and its fall, is wrapt in evil fogs and goes out at last in horrid darkness.

Wotan, the chief of this unlovely pantheon, is, says Salomon Reinach, 'at once an atmospheric, nocturnal and infernal god,' a deity of storm and of war. Only those who died a death of violence went to share his boisterous Valhalla. To him prisoners of war were sacrificed, and he was especially the god of those who were hanged, the gallows being thought of as his steed—a point for pious Nazi consideration. It was an old saying in Germany that when Wotan's wind blew someone had hanged himself. This supreme god of the North was also a black magician, versed in the darkest lore.

For a draught from Mimir's well of wisdom he bartered an eye. He was accompanied by wolves and ravens. Such 'knowledge' as he possessed is of the kind one might expect from a rather cunning and ignorant shaman in a Siverian tepee. The sacrifices offered up to him were in conformity with later Satanic practice. Wotan's 'blood-eagle' was carved upon their backs as they lay upon the altar yet alive. King Aun of Upsala sacrificed nine of his sons in turn to Wotan in order to prolong his own life. Each sacrifice gave him ten extra years of existence, and when at last his folk forbade him to yield a tenth son to the god-cannibal, he perished. Such was precisely the practice in respect of those deities who were the prototypes of the Luciferian pantheon.

Ran, the goddess of the Sea, whose name means ' Robbery,' cast her nets upon the grey ' swan's-bath ' of the Northern waters to ensnare seafarers, dragging the bodies of the drowned to her dwelling beneath the waves. In Thor, the god of Thunder, and the atmosphere, we find, perhaps, the sole spark of kindly feeling in this grim faith, the personification of the rude and slow-witted peasant, as Herr W. Golther suggested in his *Religionen und Mythen der Germanen*, although at seasons he is sufficiently furious of mien, as becomes a god of thunder. Odin's wife, Freya, was the Teutonic woman deified, blonde, and abundant, the patroness of marriage and fecundity. Much of her time appears to have been occupied in being run off with by amorous giants. Though a goddess, she was also woman, that is, the prize of the strongest, in the sight of the Blonde Beast.

But of this gang of divine ruffians, the natural deities of the S.S. and the Gestapo, none sank to such depths of murderous infamy as Loki, the very soul of perfidy and destruction, the Mercury, one might believe, of the younger school of Nazi neophytes, who must studiously have conned his adventures in duplicity and homicidal sharp practice, ' a sly, seducing villain,' as honest old Jacob Grimm described him. Like the devil, he has a limping walk, and he is certainly the German prototype of Satan or Mephistopheles. Such harm as he does, adds Grimm, is of that kind which, in Germany, is usually ascribed to the devil. Even the blood-gorged gods of the Edda bind him in chains until the end of the physical world, when he is to be released—another striking analogy with the Satanic legend. At the end of things, on the dreadful day of Ragnarök, he and his offspring, the Fenris wolf, aid the powers of darkness to overcome and destroy the gods. Like Lucifer, he is ' fair in form, evil in disposition,' a thief, liar, and master of all low cunning and knavish stratagem.

It is unnecessary, I think, to proceed further in an endeavour to make it clear that the type of religion which,

C

as we shall see, the Nazi authorities are presently cultivating in Germany, is drawn from a basis of myth so savage, primitive, and debased as to arouse shocked surprise that a people with any claim to civilization could for a moment countenance so wild and infamous a design. Gentlemen with bifurcated beards in Leipsic and Munich may writhe at such a description of their efforts to impose these ancient horrors upon the Christian faith and to graft them upon the gospel of Christ. But that is what they propose to do, nevertheless, though a number among them desire the utter extirpation of Christianity and its replacement by this gross heathenism, as I shall make abundantly clear at a later stage.

It is well known that the hero-legends of old Germany, as viewed through the music-dramas of Richard Wagner, have made a deep impression on the mind of Adolf Hitler. Indeed, it is not too much to say that *The Ring of the Nibelungs* has probably inspired him more than anything with the belief he so piously cherishes that the German people are descended from a semi-divine strain of supermen and superwomen such as he beholds stalking through the painted forests which compose the backgrounds of *Rhinegold* or *The Valkyrie.*

That Wagner's operas appear to Hitler to provide ample proof of the validity of his absurd Nordic theory is accepted in Nazi circles, and that they affect him profoundly, much as *East Lynne* was wont to affect Victorian old ladies, is notorious. In the semi-privacy of his box at the Opera, *The Ring* has been known, again and again, to reduce him to maudlin tears, so that he is compelled at times to turn from its sterner splendours and seek relief in the strains of *The Merry Widow,* Vienna's flimsiest example of *opéra bouffe.*

It seems a pity that Hitler did not scan more closely the credentials of Wagner's *dramatis personæ* before he elected to exalt them into a personal if not a national pantheon. Had he gone to those literary sources which reveal to us the pre-Wagnerian condition of these theatrically stately beings, he might not have adopted them as his official lares and penates. For those earlier records disclose the gods and heroes of *The Ring* for what they really were—low-grade savages of peculiarly unpleasant habits, cannibals, homicides and oath-breakers, monsters of cunning and immorality, so closely resembling many of his Nazi friends, indeed, that he might well have quailed at the prospect of cultivating such a choir invisible.

Most people have at least a general acquaintance with the plot and argument of Wagner's *Ring*. The Rhine maidens guard a secret hoard of gold (not marks, or even Reichmarks, which showed their good sense) which the dwarf Alberich, chief of the Nibelungs (who were not ' Nordics '), badly coveted. Alberich stole it and made a ring from it, but in time it was filched from him by the German god Wotan, who was probably the first Nazi. Wotan entrusted the bauble to the dragon Fafnir until a mortal hero should arise who should restore it to the spirits of the Rhine.

This destined hero is Siegmund, the son of Wotan by a mortal woman. His twin sister, Sieglinde, is carried off by the robber Hunding, but he slays the spoiler by the aid of the Valkyrie Brunhilde, who, because of her act, is doomed by Wotan to sleep within a circle of fire until a mortal hero shall awaken her.

This hero is Siegjroed, the son of Siegmund and Sieglinde, who disenchants Brunhilde and becomes her betrothed. But he is beguiled into wedding Gutrune, with fatal results. If we appeal to the original versions of this primitive story, however, we discover a state of things very different from the rather oleographic hero-tale.

Wagner drew his plot and its personnel from a rather extensive cycle of primitive legends about the Volsungs, the tribe to which his heroes belonged, and this he altered to suit the exigencies of his art and to glorify his subject. In the oldest version of the story Sieglinde vows a terrible vengeance againsr her abductor, murders his children, and sends her own son, Siegfried, to live in the forest with his father, Siegmund.

In order to fit themselves for the dire work of revenge, the pair of forest-dwellers ' become werwolves,' that is, they lead the lives of wolves, leaping from the woods upon passing travellers, and devouring them. Finally, in the hour of vengeance they set fire to Hunding's dwelling, and Sieglinde, seeing her vengeance completed, casts herself into the flames, exclaiming as she does so : " I have so toiled for revenge that I am no longer fit to live "—a conclusion with which most ordinary people would find themselves in hearty agreement, and which may be commended to those Nazis who would appear to have modelled their conduct upon such early Germanic prototypes as we have just been discussing.

In short, an examination of the sources of Germanic myth displays its characters as violent and malicious savages, primitive creatures of the wild, cruel and cunning in their outlook on life, and monstrous in their loves and hates. In them is nothing of the gentle and chivalrous spirit which inspires the British Arthurian romances, which are so often eloquent of high motives and tender sentiment.

But the outstanding demerit of these barbarous monsters is their capacity for ' oath-breaking.' The cunning they reveal in breaking a pledged promise in the spirit whilst preserving the letter of the same, indeed, resembles Nazi procedure so closely, that one is forced to conclude that the modern régime has drawn its inspiration from the example of the Volsungs.

Nearly every commentator of these sagas, German as well as British, lays scornful stress upon the ' slim ' and double-faced quality of the ancient Teutonic heroes. Their treachery, too is notorious. Siegfried is cheated out of his bride by her rival's mother, and is done to death by his enemy when taken unawares. Not a single page of the Volsung saga which does not reek of vengeance and drip with blood.

I think I can claim to have perused most of the world's traditional literature, but never have I encountered, even in that which describes the myths of the most abandoned savages, a spirit of cruelty so absolute, such a love of slaughter for its own sake, or a mendacity so callous and shameless as those narrated in the crabbed and unlovely pages of the German hero-tales.

And surely a race and a people who can accept and

glorify the banal abominations of the *Ring* (which stand quite apart from the beauty and wonder of its marvellous music) can possess little of the saving gift of humour. It is well known that intelligent Germans laugh at the long and tiresome recitatives of Freya, the wife of Wotan, which they have dubbed ' The curtain-lectures,' and jeer at the crass sentimentality of much of the dialogue—the snufflings of a sentimental ogre.

It may be that after the War Herr Hitler will have leisure to explore with greater faithfulness the early versions of the myths of his cherished heroes, whose conduct seems to have prompted so many of his own actions.

When at last this sanguinary paganism began to dwindle before the dawn-light of the Christian faith, its remaining ministers and adherents piously fostered it in the more remote forest-lands of old Germany. There it took on a somewhat different guise. As Grimm and other writers have made plain, its god-like shapes assumed the forms of wizards and witches, particularly the latter. For example, Hölle, or Holda, the earth-goddess, became a sorceress, the Norns degenerated into witches, Loki became the German version of the devil. In short, the divinities joined the ranks of those human sorceresses who had formerly been regarded as diviners, spae-wives, possessors of secondary vision, and became personalized as witches. The cult of witchcraft was not the remnant of their broken-down worship, as seems to be believed in some quarters, but rather a pre-existing nucleus of sorcery, perhaps of aboriginal origin, which was quickened into life and corporate activity because of their subsequent association with it.

All over Europe this process went on. The old gods became the presiding spirits of bodies of local sorcerers, some of whom were probably named after them and personified them. Thus, in various witch societies on the Continent, and in Britain, we find leaders known as Diana, Aradia, Holda, Robin Goodfellow, Satan, Christsonday, and the Fairy Queen, all of which are euphemisms for some more ancient divine title.

But with this phase of Satanism I shall deal at greater

length later on.   Here I only wish to emphasize it because of its later association with Satanism proper, which, soon after the official acceptance of Christianity in Germany, began to raise its head.

As I have already indicated, the appearance in Germany and other European countries of heretical sects, which seem to have come from the East via the Balkan Peninsula, did more to quicken the spirit of the broken-down native faiths.   The Manichæand, Bogomiles, and other Satanist bodies joined hands with the local exponents of sorcery and black magic, with the result that these, more elementary and less well-defined in their ideas, accepted the Luciferian doctrines, in which they saw the complete and sublimated principle of their own more primitive and cruder notions. At least the more ' advanced ' and ' intelligent ' of them appear to have done so, for what we know as witchcraft seems to have been the Satanism of the mob, of the folk, while Luciferianism or Satanism, as expressed by the Bogomiles particularly, was the preserve of those more exclusive ranks of society who chose to tread the path Satanic.   At the same time, we can draw no hard and fast line between these two phases of Satanism.   Their under-lying principles were the same, the ritual they employed— a blasphemous parody of that of the Roman Church— was nearly coincidental, and the ' priesthood ' or ' ministry ' of both may well have been undertaken by the same persons.   Witchcraft was the Satanism of the poor and the baser bourgeoisie ; Luciferianism was the Satanic cult of the great and powerful, and instances where the twain overlapped or commingled, as in the notorious case at North Berwick, are by no means lacking.

In Germany witchcraft certainly possessed some of the attributes of a fertility cult, that of the great earth-mother, which merely reveals that in that country it had stronger associations with the old religion of the soil than elsewhere.   But let us first look for traces of Luci-ferianism proper, for the signs of that dreadful heresy which was to have so dire an effect upon her later occult history, in Germany.   Here we must not permit any gaps in the proof, as by doing so the whole purpose and intention of this book would fail, a clear and complete continuity of record being essential to its thesis.

We discover what are perhaps the first traces of the Eastern heresy of Luciferianism in Germany in the indictment and execution of certain Cathari at Goslar in the year 1051. These Cathari, like the Bogomiles, were a sect of Manichæan origin, and the occasion of their trial was deemed of sufficient importance to call for the personal attendance of the Emperor Henry III himself. The record of their trial is brief, but all were hanged, which in itself speaks for the gravity of their offence in the eyes of the Crown. At Strasbourg, in the year 1114, so many heretics of this kind had been gathered into the local prison-house that the mob, in panic, rushed the place, laid violent hands upon them, and burned them outside the city. From that time heresy-hunts and burnings became a feature of life in the German cities. The countryside seems to have teemed with Satanists, and kings, governors, and bishops vied with each other in their extirpation.

Not only were these folk worshippers of Lucifer, the principle of evil, but anarchists in the worst sense of that somewhat obscure term, the political side of their activities being directed towards the creation of general chaos and social confusion. Rulers like Barbarossa, Henry VI, and Frederick II promulgated laws and penalties for their suppression during a century and a half, but still their propaganda persisted, and the utmost vigilance failed to destroy them.

By certain grossly biased witers these abominable sects are described as the early exponents of a Protestantism which they do not choose to distinguish from paganism. This monstrous and utterly baseless charge, the delusion of a narrow and illogical interpretation of honest doctrinal development, is proven to be false by the manner in which the Protestant Church itself dealt with Satanism and witchcraft, for, if anything, it was rather more rigorous in the punishment it meted out to diabolism than was Rome itself. And we have only to observe how the harassed remnants of both the Roman and Lutheran Churches are standing shoulder to shoulder in afflicted Germany to-day, in the fight against the new pagan uprising in that country, to realize that if the Church of Christ is to triumph it must gather the members of its universal body together in one mighty effort of resistance to the powers of Hell.

In the year 1231, Pope Gregory the Ninth, alarmed by the progress of the Luciferian sect in Germany, gave office to one, Conrad of Marburg, to take strict order against its members wherever found. He seems to have applied himself to the task with address and more than ordinary severity, but some eighteen or twenty months after his appointment, he was waylaid by Satanists near Marburg and assassinated.

Signs that in certain regions of Germany the general commonalty of the folk had been thoroughly debauched by Satanists are by no means lacking. An outstanding example of this was the condition of things amongst the Stedinger, or peasantry of the coast lying between the River Weser and the Zuyder Zee, who, as early as the eleventh century, had succeeded in casting off both the rule of their Norman and Saxon superiors and that of the Church. At first the patriarchal government of this coastal tract was benign and of good report, but by degrees the people appear to have sunk back into their ancient paganism. Here the Luciferians recognized a typical opportunity for sowing the seeds of devil-worship and anarchy, and irreligion and licence soon claimed the region for their own.

Scandalized by the conditions prevailing in Friesland, the Count of Oldenberg and the Archbishop of Bremen, with other notables, formed a league against the defaulting peasants, and at length dispatched an army against them in 1229. It was summarily defeated, and the Stedinger overran the neighbouring provinces, plundering and destroying abbeys, and committing the most outrageous desecrations. Pope Gregory launched his anathemas against them, stigmatized them as sorcerers and miscreants, and excommunicated them *en masse*.

"The Stedinger," said His Holiness, "seduced by the devil, have abjured all the laws of God and man, slandered the Church, insulted the holy sacraments, consulted witches to raise evil spirits, shed blood like water, taken the lines

of priests, and concocted an infernal scheme to propagate
the worship of the devil, whom they adore under the name
of Asmodi. The devil appears to them in different shapes—
sometimes as a goose or a duck, and at others in the figure
of a pale black-eyed youth, with a melancholy aspect,
whose embrace fills their hearts with eternal hatred against
the holy Church of Christ. This devil presides at their
sabbaths, when they all kiss him and dance around him.
He then envelops them in total darkness, and they all,
male and female, give themselves up to the grossest and
most disgusting debauchery." (13.)

Finally, almost the entire military force of North
Germany was levied to suppress the Stedinger, their
country was invaded, and they were defeated in a pitched
battle in 1234. Thousands of them were slain and their
land laid waste, and it was not until they had made penance
and given satisfactory pledges for good behaviour that the
ecclesiastical ban of excommunication was lifted two
years later.

In the year 1626 the Bishops of Bamburg and Hebron
discovered to their dismay the existence of widespread
Satanist activities in their adjoining episcopates, which
were deeply infected with the abomination of devil-
worship. By means of a well-devised propaganda the
Luciferians had succeeded in recruiting thousands to their
sacrilegious cult, and were preaching anarchy as well as
infidelity. Alarmed by the scope of this anti-Christian
movement, the Bishops convened a court of justice,
including many jurists and ecclesiastics of note and indicted
large numbers of persons of the crime of Satanism, some of
them men and women of consequence, wealthy merchants,
State senators, and priests. Furious at their arrest, the
prisoners accused the Bishop of Hebron himself as one of
their accomplices. The proceedings dragged out for nearly
four years, and during that time almost a thousand miserable wretches were sent to the stake. In the course of the
proceedings evidence was brought forward not only of the
prevalence of the most abandoned Satanic orgies, but also
of a desperate conspiracy against law and order.

As I have said, witchcraft appears to have been to some

c*

extent the more plebeian side of Satanism, the Luciferianism of the poor and the less fortunate. As regard
the origin of this particular type of Satanism, two main
theories hold the field of debate, Miss M. A. Murray, a
well-known Egyptologist, believing that it was a definite
cult, descended from the worship of some such pagan
goddess as Diana with a well-defined ritual and mode of
worship, whereas Mr. Montague Summers is of opinion
that it was the nature of mere heresy. For my own part,
I believe both of these theories contain a considerable
measure of truth, though this is scarcely the place to review
them *in extenso*, as they should be examined. Here,
indeed, it is necessary to describe witchcraft in Germany
as the 'poor relation' of Satanism, and, as such, I shall
deal with it in the next chapter.

CHAPTER IV

WITCHCRAFT, SATANISM, AND THE VEHMGERICHTE

IF the Satanism known as witchcraft had evil results in
England and Scotland and violently invaded the life of
France, its abominations shook German society to its
base. If we glance for a moment at its effects in any
given German community we at once obtain the measure
of its monstrous menace to civilization. The story to be
gleaned from the rough statistics of trial and execution in
the city of Würzburg alone for the two years from 1627 to
1629 is a terrible commentary upon the scourge of Satanism
during the first third of the seventeenth century, and, as
E. D. Hauber remarks in a note in his *Bibliotheca Magica*,
these records are by no means complete, and do not embrace
many other local burnings and executions.

In these two years no less than one hundred and fifty-
seven persons were given to the flames of Würzburg alone
for the offence of witchcraft. They were burned in batches
of five or six at a time, and were of all grades and ranks of
life, including four councillors, fourteen vicars of the Cathedral, the burgomaster's wife, an apothecary's wife and

daughter, three play-actors, four innkeepers, the children of a councillor named Stolzenberg, a young daughter and two little sons, and Göbel Babelin, the civic beauty or 'toast' of Würzburg. Others were 'folk found sleeping in the market-place,' that is tramps or vagrants. Of the thirteenth and fourteenth burnings it is recounted that the four persons then cast into the flames were 'a little maiden nine years of age ; a maiden still less, her sister ; their mother, and their aunt, a pretty young woman of twenty-four.'

Following these came, in dreadful procession, Steinacher, the richest burgher in the place, and Baunach, the most obese, as well as many another substantial citizen and matron. Before you curse the memory of their judges, as any normal person will feel inclined to do, remember that the great majority of these unhappy people were self-convicted of crimes more or less appalling, that they had come forward, of their own volition, stricken with remorse, no man accusing them, and had poured into the ears of authority tales of criminal depravity and Satanic horror which terrified their superstitious judges into condemning them out of hand.

These conditions might have been reflected in many cities in the Germany of that day. No body of men, even in 1627, was going to accuse and convict their fellow-justices of abominable crimes or hale fourteen of the local clergy to the fire, as did the councillors of Würzburg, unless they were in a state of the direst panic. No jurisdiction would have massacred innocent children simply because they were the offspring of self-confessed Satanists unless the whole community was trembling for its existence. To these people the devil was no nursery myth, as he is to millions to-day, but a very definite and awful reality. In the general opinion of the age sin was a species of disease, a pestilence which might seize upon multitudes and destroy them as surely as did the plague or cholera. Indeed, we find this notion still prevailing amongst 'backward' populations, as, for example, in south-western Mexico, where yellow fever is still worshipped as 'Uncle Fever,' and placated with gifts and sacrifices by persons who receive a State education.

As they were being consumed, these wretched creatures, old and young, shrieked out blasphemous invocations to Lucifer which appear to have. maddened their innocent fellow-citizens.   One of them ran :

'Anion, Lalle, Sabolos, Sado, Pater, Aziel,
Adonai Sado, Vagoth Agra, Jod,
Baphra ! Komm ! Komm ! '

As the flames wrapped their bodies like red winding sheets they howled this doggerel backward, invoking the demons named with terrible cries, while groans and echoing shrieks arose from the packed crowds who watched them burn. (14.)

The modern alienist would have incarcerated the whole band of Luciferians in the local Bedlam. But the apothecary's wife and daughter had sold poisons and had boasted aloud of their Satanic accomplishments. The clergy, whose duty it was to protect the people from Satan, had confessed that they had devoted them to his wrath, and others had threatened their neighbours with the direst torments and losses. For these people, it must be insisted, were not only black sorcerers, but the dreaded anarchists of their day. Their task, as they conceived it, was to lay the whole structure of human society in ashes, so that it is scarcely surprising that society retorted by dooming them to a similar fate.

These Satanists were foes to humanity at large, continually harassing and menacing their neighbours, rendering their lives miserable, poisoning them, pilfering their goods, undermining and gibing at their religion. Witchcraft was no ' delusion,' as many of its modern historians appear to have believed, but a canker in the body politic, a festering disease of envy, spite, and terrorist malice which must be excised if civilization were to endure. If in Germany it was greatly more mischievous than elsewhere, that was undoubtedly due to the prevailing spirit of that gloomy soil, which was jealous and malicious to an abnormal degree, and where the vices of personal, as well as national, pride and vainglory have from the first been remarked upon by acute observers of the race.

The Satanists known as witches in Germany were by no means confined to that type of hag who in England or Scotland appears to have been characteristic of the cult, but, as in some parts of France, were composed of the general elements of burghal society, as we have seen in the case of Würzburg. They met on heaths and commons outside the towns and cities, and after celebrating the dark mystery of the black mass, ran riot in orgies so obscenely disgusting that those who took part in them stamped themselves as belonging to that class of depraved degenerate from which the anarchist has in all times been chiefly recruited.

Those miscreants, indeed, desired nothing less than to debauch mankind and drag it down to their own level of abomination, and the punishments inflicted upon them are significant of the horror which the decent and self-respecting elements of the population felt for them. They were not only the destroyers of the fruits of industry, the saboteurs of law and order, but assassins of the soul. Thousands of the innocent or the merely unbalanced doubtless shared their fate, but one must make allowances for the panic fears which their conduct inspired, fears which are reflected in the vindictive ballad known in old Germany as the ' Druten Zeitung,' or ' The Witches' Gazette,' in which the most harrowing descriptions appeared of the sufferings of the condemned in Franconia, Bamberg, and elsewhere during the year 1627.

As early as 1484 Pope Innocent VIII inveighed against the scourge of Satanist witchcraft in the archdioceses of Mainz, Cologne, Salzburg, and Bremen with such effect that two Dominican Inquisitors were appointed to deal straitly with the abomination. These were Heinrich Krämer and James Sprenger, the joint authors of one of the most celebrated treatises on witchcraft the *Malleus Maleficarum* or ' The Hammer of the Evil-doers.' Naturally, the work is racy of the superstitions of its time but if this be discounted, it is plain from its pages that its authors most earnestly believed they were combating and unveiling not only a heresy of blasphemous and irrational origin, but also a quasi-political conspiracy, the object of which was the ultimate demolition of all law and order. (15.)

The grand meeting-place of the witches in Germany was the Blocksberg, or Brocken, in the Hartz Mountains, where the stated meetings of the order were held, and which has been rendered famous by the Walpurgis Night scene in Goethe's *Faust*. This festival was celebrated on the eve of May Day (30 April) when fires were kindled on the height and sacrifices offered, and the whole diablerie of Germany was thought of as foregathering on this peak, according to Johannes Prætorius. But Martin Luther could not believe that the witches were brought thither on the backs of goats, or bestriding broomsticks, much as he credited their other magical exploits, which were, of course, purely imaginary. It is now known that the witches carried their brooms with them to the Sabbath and that on approaching the place of rendezvous, bestrode them, leaping along and dragging the switches after them on the grass.

Nor did these malefactors keep aloof from the houses of prayer in their intention to bedevil the whole structure of society. In 1746 Maria Renata Sænger, sub-prioress of the convent of Unterzell, was proved to have been in conspiracy with the Satanists of Würzburg, who were still at their evil work. She was suspected of witchcraft because of her atheistical language and conduct, and when some of the nuns became ill and others showed signs of ' demonic possession,' it was discovered that she had drugged them with a magical draught of herbs. She was strictly examined and was found to be not only a woman of loose life and conduct, but a ' baptized ' member of the Satanist fraternity, skilled in the knowledge of poisonous drugs and simples. Night after night, she had stolen from the convent to join the local Sabbath presided over by the Grand Master of the Satanists of Würzburg, under the witch-name of Ema, so inscribed in the Black Book, or roll of this pagan band. On being accused, she exhibited the hellish fury of the Satanist. Her cell was found to contain numerous phials of poison and bundles of noxious herbs. On being urged to do so, she made a full and open confession, describing her infernal experiences and the manner in which she had gained recruits to the Satanist ranks. After trial, she was condemned to be burnt, but the sentence was commuted to one of beheading by the sword of the executioner. (16.)

The cruelty which accompanies panic was on many occasions responsible for wholesale holocausts of witch-folk in Germany, and numerous perfectly innocent persons were probably done to death along with the guilty before the flood-tide of judicial wrath and terror began to subside. It seems not unlikely that the continual public assaults, arrests, and burnings of the Satanist witches in the cities and towns of Germany had resulted in well-nigh extirpating the adherents of the Satanist cult and given pause to the hidden personages who instigated them to their anti-social work. In any case, only the *canaille* of the movement seem to have been left, its most wretched examples, when some of the foremost German princes, the Duke of Brunswick, the Elector of Menz, the Elector of Brandenburg and others, shuddering at the horrors of the torture-chamber (an evil borrowing from hell, defacing a just cause) resolved to put an end to the ghastly business in the first quarter of the seventeenth century. The number of witches arraigned almost at once diminished, showing that the sadistic feelings of executioner and popu-lace, roused to fever-heat, had been the chief factor in the arrest of hundreds of hapless folk, whose torments they hoped to gloat over.

But the righteous abolition of torture by no means put an end to the cult of Satan in Germany. In the very year in which torture was abolished in Brandenburg, Satanism broke out in Hesse with frightful violence, and a sorcery trial which terrified the whole duchy was commenced at Lindheim. The records of this are obscure, but it is known that numbers were incarcerated in a tower on the banks of the Nidder, and burned alive within its walls. Thirty years later a second witch-hunt took place in this district, when the ' King' and ' Queen ' of the witches were captured and ' died blaspheming God.' The cruelties perpetrated upon those unhappy wretches on this occasion by a soldiery typical of the country, are indescribable and at last the mob rose to put an end to the unmerciful conduct of the military, and drove them from the town.

The uniformity of the charges against the Satanist witches reveals that they practised a well-defined ritual and worship of Satan, as personified by the Sabbatic goat. This was certainly the 'Satan,' priest, or leader of the band disguised as a goat, wearing a goat's mask and hide and presiding over the proceedings. The miserable adherents of the cult were compelled to do his will in all things and at every Sabbath he called the roll of membership and exacted from each a full account of the wickedness he or she had perpetrated since the last stated meeting. To him they had to make obscene obeisances, adjure their Maker, and hearken while he read to them the commandments of Lucifer, out of a 'black book.' The apparatus of worship, black candles, black altar, and so forth, were the same as in the case of the more aristocratic Satanism and an important part of the ritual was the defilement of the host, according to the Luciferian rite. (17.)

In the year 1714 Frederick William I, the father of Frederick the Great, decided that all cases of sorcery which occurred in Prussia and which appeared to be worthy of the death penalty must be subject to his final revision and personal decision, and that no execution for this crime might take place unless the warrant for the same bore his sign-manual. That this decision marked the end of Satanism in Germany would be a quite false assumption at which to arrive.

That the great national legend of Faust is closely associated with the tradition of German diabolism cannot be doubted. The best modern study of this famous occult episode, from a literary viewpoint, comes from the pen of Mr. Charles Richard Cammell, whose researches into occult affairs are well and favourably known. (18.) He has clearly established the definite existence of a magician of that name and has disentangled the personality of the actual Faust from the associations which formerly obscured it by its confusion with lesser wizards and imposters. Johannes Faustus, or Johann Faust, taught magic publicly at the University of Cracow, but his personal story was quickly absorbed in the fogs of legend, giving rise to the English drama of Marlowe and the deathless masterpiece of Goethe, as well as to a hundred popular tales and anecdotes.

Mr. Cammell makes it clear, too, that the spirit Mephistopheles, so clearly associated by Goethe with Faust as seducer and tempter, must not be confounded with the supreme spirit of evil, but was merely a famulus or familiar, the servant of his will, as the earliest Faust Book, that printed at Frankfurt-on-Main in 1587, reveals. Mephistopheles was a subsidiary demon of the hellish host, and nothing more, the reminiscences of a Kabbalistic form, Mephiz, ' the liar.'

Faust, according to other authorities, seems to have flourished during the first half of the sixteenth century. A native of Württemberg, he studied medicine at Cracow in Poland, but his life appears to have been irregular, though we must not confound him with that Georgius Faust, or Sabellicus, a wandering necromancer, who was certainly a monster of profligacy and incidents in whose dreadful career have certainly been attributed to the genuine Faustus.

Still the figure presented in the Faust legend as a whole typifies the medieval German sorcerer. In his personality is indeed crystallized the entire tradition of German black magic. He is an adept in that Satanist cultus which manifested itself in medieval Germany so much more powerfully than in any other European country. He typifies, in the grand manner, the career and fate of the more prominent Luciferian master. Still his history is that of all Satanists—the haunting desire for personal power and dominion, the approach to Lucifer, the temptation and dreadful pact, the brief triumph and the spiritually fatal consequences—for in German tradition Faustus is lost and not saved, as in the merciful sequel of Goethe.

We must now consider certain arcane cults which appeared in Germany during the later centuries in which Satanism was rife, with a view to ascertaining how much or how little they may have influenced its spirit and ideals, or have been influenced by them. More especially must we review the history of Rosicrucianism and of the Vehm-gerichte.

'Volumes' have been written and published within recent years on the subject of Rosicrucianism, either to make it appear a valid arcane cult of the loftiest standing, or to abase it to the level of an absurd *jeu d'esprit* on the part of some medieval practical joker. Both appear to me equally fruitless, as does that other view which would give it—and with it the 'Rosicrucian' societies of to-day —a diabolical status or significance. For it is as absurd, unworthy, and suspicious to look for the Satanic every-where as it is fatuous and careless to adopt an attitude of nescience or sarcastic incredulity in respect of its genuine endeavours.

It is not so much that I wish to include some notice of the Rosicrucian movement in an account of German arcane cults that I allude to it in this place, but, because in common justice, I desire to remove from its more worthy centres the odium which certain writers have attached to it, and to show that in reality it has some claims to a more ancient and reputable origin than any-thing expressed in its Germanic legend would lead us to believe. That is not to say that I find myself in agree-ment with its ideals or cultus, either ancient or modern any more than as a humble devotee of the only true mystic-ism—that art and understanding of the Celestial, which leads to divine fellowship—I am able to identify myself with what I believe to be other offices of vain observance, either sophical, anthroposophical, or devoted to the mysteries of Endor.

Did such an order as the Rosicrucian formerly flourish, and, if so, what were its tenets and its main objects ? Those are still to be found who reply to the first part of this question affirmatively, although all close students of mystical literature are aware that from De Quincey's time to our own a quite extraordinary amount of proof has been brought to buttress the negative position. Indeed, De Quincey, in his crushing essay, and Mr. A. E. Waite, in his no less authoritative *True History of the Rosicrucians*, seemed to have given the *coup de grâce* to what many believe to have been one of the most extraordinary hoaxes in the records of human credulity. But none of those whose aim it has been to shatter the arguments of the pro-Rosicrucians appears to have sufficiently allowed for the fact that the doctrine of the Rosy Cross may have had affiliations with still older mystical societies, and that its present-day protagonists point triumphantly to the circumstance that a Rosicrucian Brotherhood still flourishes.

It is now generally agreed that the first public revelation of the Rosicrucian Order, real or imaginary, was closely connected with Lutheran propaganda. In the second decade of the seventeenth century there appeared in succession three works, obviously from the same pen, *The Universal Reformation*, *Fama Fraternitatis*, and the *Confessio Fraternitatis*, the expressed intention of which was the purification of an unrighteous and worldly age by the foundation of a society composed of the learned and the enlightened. The spirit of the time was pro-mystical, and the projector of the proposed brotherhood tempered his invitation to the world's wisdom with more than a hint of the mysterious. It was in the *Fama Fraternitatis* particularly that arcane suggestions were thrown out. It speaks of the Order of the Rosy Cross as already instituted, and narrates its inception and history.

Christian Rosenkreuz, it informs us, a man of noble descent, travelled widely in the East, and acquired its occult lore. Upon his return to Germany he established a secret society, composed first of four and afterwards of eight members, who dwelt together in ' the House of the Holy Ghost,' the location of which is not specified. Having instructed his disciples in the arcane tenets he had acquired during his Eastern travels he dispatched them on a mission of healing throughout Europe, but commanded them to foregather at the central institution annually on a given day, the word ' Rosy-Cross ' to be their watchword, and its pictured representation their sign or hieroglyph. They were, furthermore to preserve the secret of the society's existence for a hundred years. Christian Rosenkreuz died at the age of a hundred and six years, and not even his disciples knew the whereabouts of his place of burial.

But when the Order had existed for a hundred and twenty years a door was discovered in the House of the Holy Ghost leading to a sepulchral vault, where were discovered the secret books of the Order, the *Vocabularium* of Paracelsus, and a quantity of mystical apparatus. Under the altar was found the body of Rosenkreuz himself, without taint or corruption, holding in his right hand a book written on vellum in golden letters. Immediately after this narrative follows a declaration of its mysteries addressed by the Order to the world. It professed itself to be of the Protestant faith, and stated that the art of gold-making was but ' a slight object ' with its members. The House of the Holy Spirit, it says, ' though a hundred thousand men should have looked upon it, is yet destined to remain untouched, imperturbable, out of sight and revealed to the whole godless world for ever.'

The *Confessio* contains little more than general explanations upon the objects and traditions of the Order, which is therein described as having several degrees. Not only princes, nobles, and the wealthy, but ' mean and inconsiderable persons ' were admitted to its ranks, provided their intentions were pure and disinterested. The Order, we are told, possessed an esoteric language, and had accumulated more gold and silver than the whole world beside could yield. It was not, however, the mere gathering of wealth which concerned it, but philosophy and the inculcation of altruistic sentiment.

The spirit of the Order is, indeed, well illustrated by a passage from the writings of Robert Fludd, the English Rosicrucian. ' We of the secret knowledge,' he says, ' do wrap ourselves in mystery, to avoid the objurgation and importunity of those who conceive that we cannot be philosophers unless we put our knowledge to some worldly use. There is scarcely one who thinks about us who does not believe that our society has no existence ; because as he truly declares, he never met any of us. And he concludes that there is no such brotherhood, because, in his vanity, we seek not him to be our fellow. We do not come, as he assuredly expects, to that conspicuous stage upon which, like himself, as he desires the gaze of the vulgar.

every fool may enter: winning wonder, if the man's appetite be that empty way; and, when he has obtained it, crying out, " Lo, this is also vanity ! " '

Naturally, such a proclamation as the *Fama Fraternitatis* created an enormous sensation. Hundreds of scholars offered themselves, by pamphlet and otherwise, to the service of the Order, though no address appeared in its published declarations. But to none of these was any answer vouchsafed. Seemingly reliable evidence has been discovered that the author of the Rosicrucian treatises was John Valentine Andrea, a celebrated theologian of Württemberg, known also as a satirist and poet, and the suggestion has been made that his reason for the publication of them was that he sincerely deplored the wretchedness of his country consequent upon the Thirty Years' War, and hoped to remove it by the institution of such an Order as the *Fama* describes, holding out the hope of occult knowledge as a lure to the learned. That he did not avow as his own, or make any answer to the hundreds of applicants who desired to join this Order, has been critically explained as averse to his scheme.

But this ' explanation ' on the face of it is insufficient and unlikely, and takes no notice of the facts that not only did Andrea disown the writings in question, but actually joined the party of those who ridicules the Rosicrucian Order as a chimera. Moreover, he confessedly wrote *The Chemical Nuptials of Christian Rosycross*, a comic extravaganza, designed to satirize and discredit the entire Rosicrucian position. It is also manifest that the *Universal Reformation* was borrowed wholesale from the *Raguaglio di Parnasso* of Bocalini, who suffered for his faith in 1613.

The work of Bocalini, of which the *Universal Reformation* is merely a reflection, is unquestionably in the direct line of mystical profession and tradition, and is manifestly inspired by older writings, Byzantine, Gnostic, and Kabbalistic. Although Lutheran in spirit, it exhibits little or no Teutonic influence, and it therefore remains for the opponents of the reality of Rosicrucianism to show, not only that its obvious German imitation has no traditional arcane authority, but that the Italian model was not so inspired. Rome was the uncompromising foe of all occult learning, an attitude which drove the professors of the mystical into the opposing camp of Lutheranism. Nor can the serious intentions of Bocalini, and his standing as a protagonist of occult lore, be challenged ; and although his work differs slightly from the German Rosicrucian writings, internal evidence is wanting to show that it was not founded on circumstances of fact much more ancient than the Milanese himself actually appreciated. This, indeed, reopens the whole Rosicrucian question. But not only are Kabbalistic and Gnostic influences obvious in the writings of Bocalini, but others are apparent which I believe have a more or less direct bearing on the Mysteries of Egypt, and that he was in the direct line of succession as regards this particular tradition seems to me more than probable.

The truth is that Bocalini and his work are, in most books on the Rosicrucians, either not mentioned at all or are alluded to with ignorant brevity, and that unless and until the opponents of the Rosicrucian cultus succeed in showing that it had no bearing upon later Rosicrucian belief and practice, they have no title to regard it either as rootless or fraudulent. I may also add my testimony, from personal examination, that certain Rosicrucian bodies are in hands by no means unworthy, though I am bound to add that a few—and there is no homogeneity of direction —are quite as futile as anything in the lower reaches of occult belief can well be.

Another link of the ancient occult tradition of the darker cultus in Germany is provided by the records concerning the Vehmgerichte, those dread tribunals of secret justice which seem to have been founded in Westphalia at an early period. During the twelfth century the general public terror of the frightful severities and barbarities of those courts was so widespread that the east of Germany, where they chiefly functioned, came to be known as ' the Red Land.' Some writers, Lecouteulx de Canteleu, for example, assert that this society was joined at an early stage by a number of Knights Templar of German nationality, just as Freemasonry is said to have received a fresh impetus from the Templars in Scotland, and it admits of little doubt that both Templar and Masonic elements contributed to the Vehmic constitution at one time or another, if all did not derive their ideals and practice from a common source in the East. (19.)

The secret tribunals of Westphalia, known by the name of Vehmgerichte, arose during the period of lawless violence and anarchy which distracted the German Empire after the outlawry of Henry the Lion in the middle of the thirteenth century. The imperial power almost entirely lost its significance ; feudal oppression was rampant ; and a tyranny of force, nearly unexampled in its ferocity, rendered the life of the burgher and the peasant well-nigh insupportable. But the extraordinary thing is that the Vehm—in its early form, at least—bore a strongly marked resemblance to the code of the present German Nazis, which goes to show that racial predilection rather than political fashion is the basis of national movements.

The Vehm—a term derived from the old German *fem* meaning ' condemnation '—arose as if by magic, but in reality out of common consent and necessity. It was officered by men of all classes, and one of its codes, discovered at Dortmund, and the contents of which were forbidden to the uninitiated, throws some light upon its constitution. The affiliated members of the first degree were known as *Stuhlherren*, or ' lords justices,' those of the second, *Schappen*, or ' sheriffs,' and the third, *Frohnboten*, or ' messengers.' Two courts were constituted, the *Offenbares Ding*, or ' Open Court,' and the *Heimliche Acht*, or ' Secret Council.' The members generally were called *Wissende*, or ' the Wise Ones,' or initiated, and the clergy, women and children, Jews and heathens, along with the higher nobility, were exempt from its jurisdiction. The Vehm appears to have had a cipher or secret language of its own. Initial letters discovered in its writings are said to have stood for certain words, as, for example, ' s ' for stein, ' g ' for gras, and so forth. The members also cultivated secret signs by which they might know each other. At meals they turned the points of their knives towards the edge of the table and the prongs of their forks towards the centre !

The oaths by which they swore fealty to the brotherhood are said to have been of the most appalling description, but from the fragmentary notices of them we possess they were not without a certain degree of wild poetic sentiment.   Thus the brothers swore to serve the Vehm before anything that is illuminated by the sun or bathed by the rain, or to be found between heaven and earth, not to inform anyone of the sentence passed against him, and 'to denounce, if necessary, their own parents or kindred, Should they fail, they were " to be hanged seven feet higher than all others." '   Another oath, contained in the archives of Dortmund, which the candidate had to take kneeling, his head uncovered, and holding the forefinger and middle finger of his right hand upon the President's sword, makes him vow perpetual devotion to the Vehm, that he will defend it even against his own interests, against water, sun moon, and stars, the leaves of the trees, all living beings. He will uphold its judgments and promote their execution. He promises, moreover, that neither pain nor bribery, nor the ties of blood, nor ' anything created by God ' shall render him perjured to his trusts.

The procedure of the Vehm seems to have been as follows : If any lawless act was performed and the usual courts took no cognizance of the same an accusation was made by a member, and the culprit was cited to appear. If not an initiate he was summoned before the Open Court, but those affiliated with the Society possessed the privilege of appearing before the Secret Assembly.   If guilty, the initiate was at once condemned, but outsiders were permitted to appeal to the Inner Court.   Three summonses were given, six weeks elapsing between each, and if the abode of an accused person was unknown the summons was exhibited at a cross-road in his county or placed at the foot of the statue of some saint or on the wall of a wayside chapel.   Should the accused man be a knight dwelling in a fortified castle it was the duty of the *Schappen* to enter it at night under any pretence, even into the most secret chambers of the building, and do their errand.   But sometimes it was thought sufficient to affix the summons and the coin which accompanied it to the gate of the castle to inform the sentinel of the fact, and to cut three chips from the gate as a proof that the document had been duly served. It was, indeed, against the free-lances or robber-knights who abounded in Westphalia that the operations of the Vehm were chiefly directed, so that the delivery of the summons was frequently a matter of considerable danger.

A tradition exists that many of the victims of the Vehm were put to death by means of a dreadful engine known as ' the Virgin,' a bronze statue of gigantic size which stood in a subterranean vault. The doomed man was ordered to approach it and salute it with a kiss. When he touched it, it opened, displaying an interior bristling with sharp spikes and pointed blades. On the inside of each of the doors, about the height of a man's head, was a spike intended to pierce the eyes. A spring in front of this horrible contrivance propelled the victim inside, the doors closed, and he was torn to pieces by the merciless blades within, his mangled remains being dropped through a trap-door into a still more horrible machine consisting of wooden cylinders furnished with steel teeth. But Westphalia was not the only country where such instruments of fiendish ingenuity were in vogue, and it would seem that tradition in this case has applied to the memory of the Vehm all the miscellaneous horrors usually associated with the name of ' secret society.'

But from a righteously constituted tribunal which the appalling condition of Westphalia had rendered necessary for public safety the Holy Vehm degenerated into a medium of private vengeance in the hands of persons who abused the extraordinary powers committed to them. The tribunals were, indeed, reformed by Rupert, and the Regulations of Arensburg and Osnaburg modified some of the greatest abuses and restricted the operations of the Vehm. Still it continued to exist, and function in Germany, although the liberal civil institutions of Maximilian and Charles V rendered its operations unnecessary. The shadow of the society remained, and it was not until Napoleonic legislation abolished the last free court in the county of Münster in 1811 that the Vehm may be said to have finally become extinct. Even so, until the sixties of last century, certain citizens in that locality assembled secretly every year, boasting of their descent from the free judges, and indulging in a harmless ceremonial reminiscent of the procedure of the Vehmgerichte—so that only some sixty years separate the Vehm in its last phase from the Nazi dispensation, which in some of its provisions bears a close resemblance to the code which once terrorized old Germany.

Berg, Koop, Hutten, and other German writers have dealt at great length and with vast erudition on the subject of the Holy Vehm, and in England, the learned Francis Palgrave touched upon it in his *Rise and Progress of the English Commonwealth* (20), laying stress upon the antiquity of its foundation. He denied the secret character of the justiciary proceedings, but agreed in the general estimate of its mysteries of initiation and the existence of secret passwords and hand-grips. Crimes of an occult nature, he says, such as black magic, witchcraft and secret poisoning, came particularly under its jurisdiction. Indeed, he was of the opinion that it closely approximated in its ideals to early Anglo-Saxon legal forms.

But as regards its origins, he believed them to have had their rise at a period ' when the whole system was united to the worship of the Deities of Vengeance, and when the sentence was promulgated by the Doomsmen, assembled, like the Asi of old, before the altars of Thor or Woden.' It is notorious that bodies of this kind, in the latter stages of their history, invariably return to the traditions which originally animated them, and there can be little question that the Holy Vehm, in the latter phases of its history, not only partook of the nature of a secret society of the lower cultus—as the terror of its reputation reveals—but was a repository of those evil, subversive, and diabolic traditions from which the German mentality never seems to have wholly dissociated itself.

In his interesting work, *The Arcane Schools* (21), Mr. John Yarker gives it as his opinion that ' the original society was no doubt attached to the old pagan worship,' and remarks upon the interesting circumstances that the ritual of the Free Count ' has all the formula of Guild Masonry.' It cannot but be deemed that the Vehmgerichte is one of the great links—perhaps the most substantial—between the ancient arcane lore of Germany and its more modern development, and that its influence as its dark and awesome reputation reveals, was an evil rather than a beneficent one.

CHAPTER V

THE SATANIC POWER IN MODERN GERMANY

AFTER the close of the first quarter of the eighteenth century very few of the German States punished the crime of witchcraft or Satanism with death. This, however, did not mean that it had become practically extinct. Indeed, witchcraft had never become ' practically extinct ' anywhere, as those who study its current history are fully aware. But the elements of diabolism began to function somewhat differently. The world was expanding, communications had been vastly accelerated, and the far-seeing leaders of the Satanist power realized that mere local agitation by no means constituted the royal road to that universal chaos and international confusion which they so fanatically sought.

Just as they had wrought among the arcane societies of Greek Alexandria many centuries before with such marked success, they now cast about for suitable openings among the mystical brotherhoods of Europe, and speedily found them. I must not be conceived here as meaning that they deliberately connived with the personnel of these societies, many of which were led and composed by men of the highest ideals, full of selfless ambitions for humanity. Their *modus operandi* was rather one of interpenetration and sophistication. Cautiously and gradually they introduced their skilful and highly trained agents into the lodges and inner alcoves of the more flourishing mystical brotherhoods, until at last they achieved such a measure of authority that they were enabled to use them as instruments for the commission of their own anti-social purposes.

The body to which they first turned their attentions in Germany was one admirably suited to their purposes. In Germany, Freemasonry had assumed that peculiar phase of the pseudo-mystical which invariably attracts persons of romantic psychic tendencies, who, as a rule, are not blessed, or cursed, with political insight. It is hardly necessary to say that British Freemasonry has from the first stood aloof from all official and fraternal association with Continental Freemasonry, which it regards not only as a doctrine of vain observance, but as a political force. This I merely mention, to make plain that what I have to say here in no way reflects upon British Freemasonry, which differs as much from the Continental form as it is possible for two systems to differ in their general outlook.

The manner in which the Satanist caucus succeeded in gaining an almost complete ascendancy in the councils of the German Freemasons is best exemplified, perhaps, by the steps taken by Frederick the Great, while still Crown Prince of Prussia, to transform the fraternity into a medium for his own designs. The process has been described by more than one writer, but whereas most authorities have believed Frederick to have made Freemasonry the instrument of his purpose to enlarge the power of Germany and overthrow France, they have failed to observe that in so doing he was in his turn merely the creature of the Satanic power, which, indeed, diverted his Germanic ambitions into the current of its anarchial intention in the same manner that it is presently doing in the case of Adolf Hitler.

Frederick was initiated into Freemasonry in 1738. On his accession to the throne, two years later, he began to found lodges broadcast, and in 1740, through the agency of Von Marschall, a German Freemason, he founded the Order of Templarism in Paris. Shortly afterwards there appeared in Paris a second German emissary, Von Hundt, who alleged that his visit was made for the purpose of his initiation into the Order of the Temple by Prince Charles Edward, the Jacobite claimant. This was later proved to be a falsehood, and Von Hundt, in confusion, blurted out that he had been sent to Paris by ' Unknown Superiors' functioning from ' a hidden centre.' It seems that he had tried to enlist Prince Charles Edward in the Templar

Order under the plea that it would assist him to regain the British throne, but that he had failed to do so. (22.)

It took Von Hundt nearly ten years to get his new Masonic order placed upon a sound footing, which goes to show the persistence with which the scheme was organized and carried out.   When at last it was fully established he named it : ' The Order of the Stricte Observance.'   It was officered exclusively by men of German race, chiefly Prussian cabinet ministers, and led by Frederick himself, but, according to its own official statements, its real superiors were ' unknown persons whose names might not be divulged.'   The fact is also alluded to by Mirabeau in his *History of the Prussian Monarchy*, and he even mentions one of these agents by name, one Johnston, who later died in a German prison.

Indeed, the artificial and mendacious character of this Order of the Temple is proved by Von Hundt's statement that he was in possession of the true secrets of the Knights Templar, handed down from the fourteenth century, and linked in tradition with the Masonic legend that the Templars founded the Rose Croix degree in Scotland shortly after the Battle of Bannockburn !   With all due deference to Masonic susceptibilities, and to a time-honoured legend, anyone conversant with Scottish history will have no hesitation in stamping this tale as being among those myths one would like to be true—so that the documents which Von Hundt offered as the proofs of the authenticity of his statement must have been, as more than one authority has suggested, the most manifest of forgeries—in fact, very much ' made in Germany.'   The whole thing was, indeed, a typical trumped-up piece of Teutonic ' sensation-romance,' the kind of thing, in short, which would appeal to the beglamoured and infantile German imagination.

That the ' hidden superiors ' of the Order were, however, no myth, is certain, and that they were Satanists is also clear enough.

Frederick the Great had still ten years to reign when Adam Weishaupt (1748–1830), a Bavarian professor, founded the Order of the Illuminati in 1776.   It is by no means evident whether this society was at first in league with the Order of Stricte Observance or otherwise, but for certain reasons which will grow clearer as we proceed, I am of opinion that it was not. Indeed, it is difficult to believe that Frederick, who was, after all, merely the clever and unsuspecting tool of the Satanist caucus and certainly no anarchist so far as his own Kingdom of Prussia was concerned (however much he may have wished to bring about anarchy in France), could have allied himself with a body which was in secret the most profanely anarchical in all history.

The immediate origins of Illuminism are obscure. Some French authorities profess to find them in the doctrines of Manichæism carried to Europe by a certain Danish merchant who had lived for many years in Egypt. One English writer, quoting a French authority, even goes so far as to assert that this apostle of Manichæism was probably that thrice-mysterious Althotas, who is said to have been the master in magic of Cagliostro, and who appears in the pages of Dumas' entertaining *Memoirs of a Physician*. Althotas may or may not have been an actual personage, but it will require much more research than has been expended upon the records concerning him to make him the father of Illuminism. Time and examination may reveal, however, that he was one of its ' hidden superiors.'

But that the roots of Illuminism are to be found in Manichæism it is not necessary to doubt. Every page of the writings of Weishaupt are eloquent of the belief in the virtue of evil, that perverted morality which sees the highest good in evil, and which typifies Satanist doctrine. Weishaupt pretended that his doctrines were derived from Persian Zoroastrianism, or fire-worship, but that he knew little or nothing about this venerable Persian faith and everything about that of Manichæism is patently obvious— as clear, indeed, as that he was a scoundrel of glib and subtle genius, absolutely innocent of principle and the love of truth.

Perceiving that his ' Zoroastrianism ' was not sufficiently attractive for his purpose, he imported a vague and garbled admixture of Christianity into his cult, thus forestalling the stratagem of Alfred Rosenberg, the present-day Director of Culture of the Nazi Reich, by a hundred and sixty years. By doing so he attracted many thousands of reputable persons to his Order, and rendered it 'respectable.'

The literature and propaganda of this Order are rich in mysterious phraseology, the language of the false mystic born, but all this high-falutin rodomontade bears little relation to its authors' theories and intentions, which are now apparent to everyone in their crude nihilism. Weishaupt's scheme, indeed, was a simple one enough. It was to overturn human society, to create chaos, to deliver the earth and all that was in it over to the debased, the brutal, and the evil. His proposals, according to Henri Martin, embraced the abolition of property, social authority, and nationalism, and to bring about the return of humanity to pristine ignorance and simplicity. Blanc, in his *History of the French Revolution*, alludes to him as 'one of the deepest conspirators who have ever lived.' At a later date he threw overboard his 'altruistic' creed, and declared himself in his private correspondence as a nihilist of the most uncompromising mark, although he continued to represent Illuminism as full of saving grace for a tortured and enslaved humanity.

In Continental Freemasonry, Weishaupt, like Frederick the Great, found a convenient and accommodating medium for the dissemination of his doctrines. He was, as Mirabeau states in his *History of the Prussian Monarchy*, a member of a Masonic Lodge at Munich, the associates of which, weary of 'the hopeless outlook' presented by pure Masonic belief, resolved among them to interpenetrate and sophisticate Masonry by another system to which they gave the title of the 'Order of the Illuminati.' The very name is of Manichæan origin, as the Abbé Barruel declared. From the moment of its inception until the whole land of France lay in social and administrative ruin, the miscreants who wielded the destinies of this evilly inspired fraternity held not their hands, nor spared humanity, until their fell work was accomplished.

I am not of those who believe that a large measure of

revolutionary change in France was unnecessary. France, the brilliant exemplar of civilization, was sick unto death of internal maladies which called for the aid of a judicious social surgery. But such 'revolution' as she so sadly required was capable of achievement by gradual development, and that such a process was actually in existence one does not now require to prove. It was at this juncture, when a happy issue from her perplexities might have been expected, that the forces of hell, led and inspired by Germanic Illuminism, seized upon their opportunity and flooded her councils, her committees, her Masonic lodges, every department of her social life, with the poison of anarchy, driving to frenzy and nihilist insanity her over-wrought masses and her hysterical intelligentsia, in whom the bizarre and 'fashionable' nature-communism of Jean Jacques Rousseau had aroused a frenzy of desire for a mock-primitive existence in an artificial dream-world of patriarchial bliss.

That Weishaupt regarded Freemasonry as *une chose d'absurde* is as plain from his personal writings and correspondence as that Frederick the Great looked upon it as 'child's play,' as he described it. This, of course, was the cynicism of the Luciferian. For Weishaupt, as for the Nazi 'thinkers,' as we shall see, Christ was merely a Communist, whose gospel was pure reason, a revolutionary leader, a 'Hitler-figure,' as Dr. Wilhelm Kusserow, Vice-President of the Nordic Faith Movement, would term him. How these destructively inspired men resemble each other throughout the ages in intention and expression ! Nor is this resemblance by any means accidental. It is the result of a very definite tradition. The Christian element in Illuminism, wrote the Baron von Knigge, one of its most ardent supporters, is 'a pious fraud.' One day, he added, the Order would reveal the true origin of 'all religious lies.' That, indeed, is precisely what the leading protagonists of Nazi paganism flatter themselves they are doing to-day.

And exactly as did the Nazi pagan caucus, as we shall see, Illuminism succeeded in banishing religious teachers from the professorships of the German universities, placing its clerical members in " good benefices ' and its teachers in the schools and other centres of education. Weishaupt worked in the dark. He impressed his followers with the need for concealment, so that even to the last he remained almost unknown as a prime agitator. He insisted that the young must be drawn into his movement. These must be ' engaging, intriguing and adroit.' But evil attracts its kind, and in 1780 we find him writing that the members of his Order at Munich are ' a collection of immoral men, of whoremongers, liars, debtors, boasters and vain fools ' —the prototypes, one might suggest, of a later régime which was also to reveal itself as the dupe of Satanism.

Von Knigge, in one of his letters, unveils the persecutions of the Illuminati. ' I have written,' he says, ' against ex-Jesuits and Rosicrucians, persecuted folk who never did me any ill, cast the Stricte Observance into confusion . . . .' and, evidently conscience-stricken, he goes on to inveigh against Weishaupt as a dangerous and unprincipled persecutor and secret tyrant. The confessions of the Illuminati and the publication of their methods in the writings and papers seized by the Bavarian Government on the suppression of the Order in 1785, and published under the title of *The Original Writings of the Order of the Illuminati*, at Munich in 1787, reveal the true nature of one of the most vindictively deliberate conspiracies against human well-being in the history of the world.

Mrs. N. H. Webster, who is one of the most painstaking and well-equipped authorities on this period of occult history—though none too sympathetic to the occult standpoint—remarks in her significant book, *Secret Societies and Subversive Movements* (23), that she does not see in Illuminism a ' conspiracy to destroy Christianity, but rather a movement finding its principal dynamic force in the ancient spirit of revolt against the existing social and moral order,' or, as de Luchet has it : ' The system of the Illuminés is not to embrace the dogmas of a sect, but to turn all errors to its advantage, to concentrate on itself everything that men have invented in the way of duplicity and imposture.'

The first contact made by the Illuminists with any

D

Masonic body was that effected with the Order of Stricte Observance. This section of Freemasonry, as we have seen, was a body of almost purely German composition, although it would appear to have had an earlier French prototype and may have been a resurrection of this older fraternity, revived *ad hoc* by Frederick and his coadjutors. In any case, it was German-controlled and functioned in Germany as well in France. The go-between in this unhappy mystical marriage between a none too reputable order subversive of French Freemasonry and the wholeheartedly malicious sodality of Weishaupt was that Cagliostro, who was perhaps the greatest imposter in an age populous with empirics and false mystics. His adventures, only to be equalled, perhaps, by those of his brother picaresques Gil Blas and Casanova, as examples of a diverting blackguardism which almost overlapped the criminal, might merely have been amusing had they not been fraught with consequences so tragic to a hapless France. For there is no doubt that Joseph Balsamo, to give him his proper name, assuredly possessed that sense of the theatric which accompanies a love of occultism of a certain kind. Not only so, but it must be granted that his psychic powers were by no means feeble, and that the occult knowledge he displayed could only have come to him through initiation, though, it must be added, from initiation of no very reputable kind.

Cagliostro, who was a member both of the Order of Stricte Observance and of the Illuminati, speedily forged the bond between them at the behest of Weishaupt, as he confessed at a later juncture. Weishaupt, for his part, pushed on with his propaganda, and with the object of bringing matters to a head, convened a congress of occultists, Freemasons, mystics and pseudo-mystics, at Wilhelmsbad in July 1782, at which, says Mirabeau, the chief object of discussion was ' what is the real object of the Order and its true origin ? '

The truth is, Continental Freemasonry, so far as its more reputable elements were concerned, was fumbling in that darkness which precedes occult initiation. It had not, unhappily, turned, as did British Freemasonry, to the corridor on the right hand, which at last might have brought it to the light, but was being jostled, with demonic roughness, to that on the left, which leads to the abyss.

A second conference, held at Paris in February 1785, and convened by the members of the Rite of Philatethes, a perfectly praiseworthy body of amateur mystics of good report, but unnaturally avid for forbidden lore of a rather highly coloured kind, attracted the whole rascaldom of the lower occultism, the 'grey,' and dubious German plotters of the Stricte Observance, the mounteback Cagliostro, certain Kabbalists, and even Mesmer, the empirical hypnotist, whose art was then regarded as of supernatural origin, as well as many a worthy seeker after truth. But, as might have been expected, these conflicting elements did not coalesce.

Then the first dastard blow for revolution was struck in the monstrous affair of the Diamond Necklace, carried out by the infamous Balsamo-Cagliostro to the detriment of the fair fame of the innocent Marie Antoinette. That this vile plot was the express act of the Order of the Illuminati, working through their villainous tool Cagliostro, is undeniable. No need to rehearse the drama of that black complot, the result of which did more to undermine the public confidence in law and order than anything in the dread history of the French Revolution.

The Congress met again in 1786, at Frankfurt this time, and under more secret auspices, and there can be no doubt that on this occasion it was agreed to loose the whole tempest of revolutionary fury upon a France now ripe for anarchy because of the social distractions which encompassed it. Well might this Congress be convened in the strictest secrecy, for it was now composed of outlaws. Some months before, a messenger of the Illuminati had sustained serious injuries in a thunder-storm while on his way to a lodge at Breslau, and the papers he carried were scrutinized. In the result, the private houses of some of the, Illuminati received a visit from the Bavarian police incriminating evidence of conspiracy was discovered, and the Order of the Illuminati was officially suppressed.

But only outwardly, superficially. According to Mrs. N. H. Webster, to whose remarks on this particular period any writer on this subject is compelled to have recourse because of their definitive character, Illuminism was only temporarily disconcerted by this disfranchisement and proceeded on its evil course for several subsequent decades (24.) In the first instance it functioned under the cloak of alliance with the Amis Réunis in Paris, with which it had amalgamated in 1771, and which was chiefly made up of pseudo-mystics of Martiniste origin and was of 'Androgyne' composition, embracing persons of both sexes and mainly of fashionable station. It also appears to have had close associations with that order known as the Grand Orient, instituted in 1772 by a dancing-master named Lacorne who had fomented disturbance in the Grand Lodge of France, and had, with a numerous following, set up this rival Masonic dispensation, which later contrived to have itself reunited with the parent body. By the early days of 1789 the greater number of the lodges of Grand Orient had been interpenetrated by the Illuminati.

The entire resources of this occult opinion, by no means negligible socially and authoritatively, were thus brought within the power of Illuminism, in which it saw nothing derogatory to the fashionable humour and inclination of the day for a return to an amiable 'patriarchal' code of primitive life and freedom, its hare-brained membership never even suspecting that it had become not the associates of a brotherhood desirous of furthering an honest liberalism, but the instrument of the Satanic purpose.

We are not here concerned with the history of the French Revolution, but with the manner in which it was precipitated by Luciferian conspiracy, employing as its tools German political cunning and the French craze for the Adamic existence rendered vacantly fashionable by the visionary and romantic 'reformer' Jean Jacques Rousseau. In 1789 the chief emissary of Illuminism in France was that 'Anacharsis' Clootz, otherwise the Prussian Baron Jean Baptiste de Clootz, a disciple of Weishaupt and an Illuminist, who pressed forward the ideal of a universal human republic and styled himself 'the personal enemy of Jesus Christ.' Haranguing the French Army, he adjured them, if Germany invaded France, to cast away their arms and embrace the Teuton invaders—thus posing as the German deliverer of France, as do the Nazis, those 'liberators' of Europe.

But France had not entered the danger-zone without receiving due warning. As Mrs. Webster indicates, many French Freemasons knew little or nothing of the Illuminist connection, the lodges containing only twenty-seven Illuminist initiates. The most whole-hearted supporters of the movement were men belonging to the upper classes and even to the royal families of Europe, numbering among them no less than thirty princes, reigning and non-reigning. Cardinal Caprara, Apostolic Nuncio at Vienna, gave due warning to Rome of the true state of affairs in Germany when he wrote in 1787 : 'The danger is approaching from all these senseless dreams of Illuminism . . . visionaries have their time, the revolution they forbode will have its time also.'

In 1789 the Marquis de Luchet wrote : 'Deluded people . . . learn that there exists a conspiracy in favour of despotism against liberty, of incapacity against talent, of vice against virtue, of ignorance against enlightenment. . . . This society aims at governing the world. . . . Its object is universal domination. This plan may seem extraordinary, incredible—yes, but not chimerical . . . no such calamity has ever yet afflicted the world.' (25.) In a word, the French Revolution carried out the purposes of Weishaupt to the letter. It realized the Luciferian ideal. It was hell let loose.

In his *History of the Jacobites* De Langres quotes a remarkable utterance of Mirabeau's. Speaking of his fellow-revolutionists in the great French debacle, the grotesque creature bellowed : 'The sect uses the people as the flesh of revolution, as good material for brigandage, after which it seizes the gold and abandons generations to torture. It is, truly, the code of hell.' De Langres proceeds to show that behind this 'code of hell' was a secret Convention, 'an occult and terrible power of which the ordinary Convention became the slavish instrument, and which was made up of the leading initiates of Illuminism. It was a power above Robespierre.' (26.)

"What," asks Mrs. Webster, "was the aim of this occult power? Was it merely the plan of destruction that had originated in the brain of a Bavarian professor twenty years earlier, or was it something far older, a live and terrible force that had lain dormant through the centuries, that Weishaupt and his allies had not created, but only loosed upon the world? The Reign of Terror, like the outbreak of Satanism in the Middle Ages, can be explained by no material causes—the orgy of hatred, lust, and cruelty directed not only against the rich, but still more against the poor and defenceless, the destruction of science, art, and beauty, the desecration of the churches, the organized campaign against all that was noble, all that was sacred, all that humanity holds dear, what was this but Satanism? In desecrating the churches and stamping on the crucifixes the Jacobins had in fact followed the precise formula of black magic." (27.)

But one prominent member of the Stricte Observance was sufficiently honest to call for its suppression when the evil work which that organization of catspaws had sponsored had at last become apparent. This was the Duke of Brunswick. In 1794 he issued a manifesto to the lodges, pleading that 'the curtain should be drawn aside.' 'A great sect,' he says, 'arose, which, taking for its motto the good and the happiness of man, worked in the darkness of conspiracy to make the happiness of humanity a prey for itself. . . . They founded the plans of their insatiable ambition on the political pride of nations. . . . They began by casting odium on religion. . . . They deluded the most perspicacious men by falsely alleging different intentions. . . . Indomitable pride, thirst for power, such were the only motives of this sect.' (28.)

Had the virtuous and well-intentioned Duke been writing of the Nazi dispensation of to-day, could his words have been any less appropriate? They could not, because the gospel and programme of the Illuminati and the Nazi miscreants is one and the same, and proceeds from the same source—the heart of hell, as all their dire and destructive acts bear witness. The Nazis are the direct descendants of the Illuminati in spirit and actuality.

For the Illuminati were by no means dispersed. Weishaupt himself functioned as a Satanist agitator for many years—indeed, he survived till 1830, dying at the ripe age of eighty-two. After the Reign of Terror, Freemasonry flourished exceedingly in France under Napoleon and there exist good proofs that Weishaupt was still seeking to interpenetrate it. (29.) Whatever complexion government took, whether Royalist, Republican or Socialist, this insatiable nihilist lay in wait to destroy it. To him the political or spiritual aspirations of his fellow-men were humane absurdities. His one ambition was the utter and final overthrow of all human social effort, the reign of Lucifer and of chaos.

In his striking book *The War of Anti-Christ with the Church and Christian Civilization*, written as long ago as 1881, Monsignor Dillon foreshadows the fruits of Weishaupt's demonic policy as follows:

> 'Had Weishaupt not lived, Masonry might have ceased to be a power after the reaction consequent on the French Revolution. He gave it a form and character which caused it to outlive that reaction, to energize to the present day, and which will cause it to advance until its final conflict with Christianity must determine whether Christ or Satan shall reign on this earth to the end.' (30.)

By far the best proof that Illuminism actually survived is provided by the report of François Charles de Berckheim, special Commissioner of Police at Mayence in 1814, and now in the Archives Nationales of France. This report is summarized by Mrs. Webster (31), and in these pages I can only find space to compress it into a paragraph or so. Roughly, Berckheim's findings are as follows: Illuminism in his day was still flourishing. 'It is becoming a great and formidable power, and I fear, in my conscience, that kings and peoples will have much to suffer from it unless foresight and prudence break its frightful mechanism.' No truer prophecy was ever penned. Furthermore, he discovered that a 'great number of initiates into the mysteries of Illuminism' were to be found at Heidelberg. Those men wore a gold ring which contained a secret motto, disclosed by the pressure of a spring, and which read : ' Be German, as you ought to be.' I was once offered one of these rings in a second-hand jeweller's shop in Edinburgh.

Illuminism, he continues, was then to be found in ' hot-beds ' all through south Germany. It was subversive of all authority. Freemasonry was merely its instrument and cloak. Its methods were extraordinarily secretive. It evidently worked on the modern system of ' cells,' each member initiating selected recruits. Its oaths of loyalty were reminiscent of the terrible pacts of the Vehmgerichte. It sought to attract likely members by means of social *salons* and similar gatherings. Its general organization was apparent. It was chiefly anxious to influence professors, literary folk, and the intelligensia, especially imaginative young men. The minds of those youths it did its utmost to debauch and convert to its anti-social principles by every means in its power. Even the Scriptures were employed ' as a vehicle for their baneful insinuations.'

The German Tugenbund, ' The League of Virtue,' says Berckheim, was derived from the Illuminati. This dangerous association, which flourished mightily in Germany at the beginning of the nineteenth century, was most certainly the source and origin of the Pan-German Movement of later times, as well as the begetter of the Alta Vendita, the directorate of the infamous Cardonari in Italy. (32.) So that we have here contemporary proof of a direct link between the Illuminati and the Nazi Party, through the ' ancestral forms ' of the Tugenbund and Pan-Germanism.

And who can doubt that the numerous Pan-German secret societies which flourished all over Germany prior to the rise of the Nazi Party, and which have been absorbed in it, did not cheirsh and foster the seeds of Illuminism, at least so far as their leaders and secret initiates were concerned ? Practically every one of these derive from the Tugenbund, which was directly the offspring of Illuminism. Of these the Ostmarkverein, ' The Eastern Frontier Association,' which was supposed to foster German sentiment on the borders of Russia, was notoriously secretive and occultly directed by hidden leaders, and had a weird and theatrically designed ritual behind it.

Similarly the Orgesh, or Einwohnerwehr, which gave so many members to Nazism, and which was founded by Escherich, had its headquarters at Munich and was composed of armed Bavarian ex-soldiers for the most part. (33.) The 'Consul' club, known as 'Organization C,' founded by Captain Ehrhardt, was the source of the infamous S.A., and a notorious instrument of assassination, harbouring ruffians of the lowest character. All of these bodies, without exception, are known to have been governed by hidden leaders, their ostensible chiefs being merely the puppets of concealed agents, who provided them with funds and dictated their policy.

That the spirit and tradition of Illuminism still flourishes in Germany to-day, and that it has fully succeeded in penetrating and sophisticating the Nazi code and philosophy, is beyond question. The insignia of its exoteric intentions are to be descried on almost every page of Nazi literature, especially those which deal with the New Pagan Movement in Germany, to the consideration of which we must now turn our attention.

CHAPTER VI

THE NAZI PAGAN DOCTRINE

THE treachery and inhumanity of Adolf Hitler have passed into the sphere of proverb. Indeed, I may say quite simply that I find it impossible to believe that any man, out of his own native and personal wickedness, could have been aroused to the perpetration of crimes so unmeasured in their atrocity upon the hapless millions of Europe as he in his frenzy has performed. The monstrous deeds carried out by his orders surely surpass the limits of human iniquity. It is true that we have records of slaughter, rapine, and cruelty of equal atrociousness in the descriptions of Hunnish invasion and in accounts of similar savage visitations. But since the period nominally fixed as the beginning of civilization, no leader or

D*

conquering potentate has revealed such a delirium of homicidal resolve or such a mania for persecution equal to or even approaching that of this wicked and merciless man.

Civilized opinion is still so appalled by the sheer horror of the tale of Nazi crime that it has not yet been enabled to visualize its abominations in true perspective. The rehearsal of these outrages is unnecessary. Every heart in civilized Europe and America is still incandescent with the wrath and shame they have engendered, and again and again they have been justly compared, in the first flush of horrified realization, with the Apocalyptic terror, which is, indeed, the only measure we have by which to estimate them.

All this may appear a trifle redundant, but in the statement of it I have a very definite purpose. For I deny that this ebullience of fiendish frenzy bears any relationship to human conduct. No man in his senses will believe that a people in the forefront of civilization, whose achievements in the realm of culture have done so much for mankind, has, by its own volition, embarked upon an orgy of what is undoubtedly demoniac fury because of a national lust for vengeance alone. That the Germans are an unnaturally arrogant and resentful people with a quite absurd belief in their superiority to the rest of humanity cannot be denied. Throughout their whole history they have evinced a barbarous cruelty and stupid mercilessness toward their enemies which has given them an evil repute for callous ferocity. But on this occasion the measure of their wrath and vindictiveness has surpassed anything previously recorded of them to such an extent as to give the impression either that they are communally insane, or that their collective sense of reason and human decency has been utterly debauched by some agency external to them and to humanity.

Had Great Britain been defeated in the Great War, there can be no question that she would have had to face peace conditions a hundred times more grievous and rigorous than those imposed upon Germany by the Treaty of Versailles, and that any opportunity of recovering her position would permanently have been denied her. Resentment of the keenest sort she certainly would have felt and displayed, but that a fury so insensate would have seized upon her as has been manifest in the case of Germany is unthinkable, nor, had she succeeded in restoring herself so far as to be able to defeat her neighbour in a subsequent contest, would she have borne herself with such savage and implacable rancour as Germany has revealed in Poland. France, with all her native irascibility, has never exhibited such an unrestrained desire for the persecution of her traditional foe as Germany has for her and for her late ally, rigorous as were her terms at the peace of 1919. None, indeed, of the more luckless States of Europe have so comported themselves in defeat as Germany has done.

No, there is something here which cannot be accounted for by the vagaries of human conduct and the natural, if wretched, desire for retribution alone. It is admitted that the present generation of German youth has been brought up to regard vengeance as its birthright, that it has been inured to a callous disregard of human feeling. But there is an iciness of purpose evident in the philosophy which underlies Nazi preparation which excludes from consideration anything so wholesome as honest human indignation or the wish to justify the national military honour. It differs from the mere fanaticism of outraged nationality as does Antarctic frost from tropic heat. The intention to wreak woe and universal outrage upon humanity in general, wherever it is placed at its mercy on sea or land, and irrespective of nationality and circumstances which the Nazi purpose reveals, is suggestive not of Germanic intention, flagrantly barbarous as that can be, but of the insanity which has its source in an environment extraordinary to that of mankind. It may be brought against this view that outrages as monstrous as any which this war has witnessed were inflicted on the innocent in the course of the Great War, and that would be perfectly true. But the same ice-cold purpose to bring final ruin upon the entire population of Europe, to enslave it utterly and to destroy the Christian faith within its bounds was certainly not then apparent. At the same time, the first latter-day associations of Germany with discarnate evil were certainly visible during the course of the Great War in countless acts of isolated ferocity, and it was only too evident that the powers of wickedness were then working in association with certain elements in Germany.

Let us consider the development and nature of the mentality which, inspired by Satanic agency, has conceived and precipitated this fatal and cataclysmic series of events.

Adolf Hitler, it may be said at once, bears all the marks and insignia of the false mystic. In this essentially commonplace-seeming man are to be found certain of the elements and attributes of the mystic, yet not in such strength or excellence as to enable him to be classed as other than a pseudo-mystic, a species of hybrid between the genuine mystic and the inferior man of the lower stamp and nature. It is from spirits of this dubious and equivocal admixture, the mulattoes or half-breeds of the mystical race, that the world's most dangerous types are forthcoming.

On one side of his nature Adolf Hitler appears as a national saviour and deliverer of the German race, as the keen-sighted seer who not only prophesies for her great triumphs and aggrandizements but who is also the devoted leader of his people, ascetic, self-sacrificing, unresting in their sacred cause. On the other he is revealed as a tyrant and implacable monster whose hands are thicker than themselves with the blood of unoffending populations whom he has mowed down by the aid of his fanatical mechanized myriads, the unrelenting escheater of the rightful territory of others, the brigand of their goods and wherewithal, the faith-breaker unsurpassed.

The truth is that Hitler is a rather ignorant and slightly educated man who has little or no personal culture, who dislikes intellectual pursuits and people, and who has only a rough smattering of knowledge concerning foreign affairs. It must be granted, however, that he is politically acute and that his powers of organization are high. In race, he is almost certainly a Slavonic Bohemian or Czech, or at least the Slav blood triumphs in him, as his physiognomy and temperament reveal. As Hindenburg realized, there is little that is Teutonic in Hitler. The old Field-Marshal dubbed him ' that *verdammt* Bohemian corporal,' which was as much as to say that he recognized the Slavonic vein in his unruly colleague's character and general make-up.

For, as is shown by the characteristic moods which chiefly govern him, Hitler is much more Slav than Teuton. These alternate between a false *bonhomie* and gloomy, withdrawn silence. The ordinary *petit bourgeois* half of him is shrewd, cautious, and politically hard and cunning, while the other and mystical, or rather pesudo-mystical half of his spirit is continually wafting him away into strange realms of his own creation. For, like all persons of mystical temperament, he has conjured up a paradise where he may find refuge from the more material considerations of every day.

In the case of a great and genuine mystic, his conception of such a half-way house betwixt earth and heaven is not coloured by his personal desires, but appears as a place of divine rapture, a holy of holies, a personal sanctuary. It is notorious, however, that where a spiritual *metis*, or half-caste, of the type of Adolf Hitler is concerned, this bridge betwixt the planes of the material and the terrestrial is apt to become merely a series of pontoons for the march of his personal ambitions and hopes, rather than a heavenly isthmus approaching that paradise toward which the true mystic strains.

In Hitler's case it becomes the bridge Bifröst of Teutonic mythology. The prime cause of his visionary moods and temporary withdrawals is that tumultuous Wagnerian inspiration which has gained almost supreme dominion over him. For him, as for many other Germans, the sensuous and victoriously intoxicating music of Richard Wagner induces a rhapsodic condition of that kind which has been so admirably described by a French metaphysician as *Folies des splendeurs*. It transports him not to a sphere of noble ecstasy and spiritual exhilaration, as it certainly does in the case of many people, to whatever country they may belong, but rather to the Germanic Valhalla, where the gods and demigods of the ancient Teutons, his idols and the objects of his racial worship, await him, and where he may breathe an atmosphere of Germanic superiority, and revel in triumphant meditations of conquest and vengeance over the lesser breeds who have offended against the sanctities of Teutonic majesty.

This inheritance of ' oleographic ' and grandiose vision he would appear to have received from his mother, Klara Poelzl, the dreamy peasant girl who ran away from her native village to Vienna at an early age. To the richly gloomy folk-beliefs of her Austro-Czech frontier home she added, during a ten-years' residence in the great city, a feverish hero-worship for the music-dramas of the Master of Bayreuth, which appeared to her as the spiritual apotheosis of her native legends. During his boyhood, Adolf Hitler was practically her sole companion, as she lay house-bound, and latterly bed-bound, in the long affliction of cancer, and from her lips he received that initiation into the hero-tales of his native region which inspired him with a fierce and overmastering desire to achieve world-dominion for the German folk.

That the defeat of Germany induced in a young man so inspired the wildest despair is scarcely a matter for surprise. Adolf Hitler, the imaginative corporal, saw all his idols go down in a day. That Germany which he had believed to be invincible was crushed and broken, bereaved of the fruits of her previous victories, of her colonies, of her honour, doomed to what he believed to be a shameful peace. Like thousands of other Germans, he looked wildly around for scapegoats. The Jews, the Socialists, the Pacifists had stabbed the sacred Fatherland in the back. First, vengeance upon these, next upon the exulting French, who were already lording it in the Ruhr, then, last of all, upon that detestable English race which had ever been the sworn enemy of those warrior peoples who found it necessary to widen their territories by the noble conquest of the sword. The resurrection of Germany became an obsession with the now disbanded soldier. The thought of the ' wrongs ' of his adopted country induced in him such a tempest of fury that for months, it seems, he was unable to address himself to the common tasks of life.

It is at such seasons of wrath and bitter despair that the diabolic influence, ever on the watch for new and desperate converts, seizes upon its opportunities. The mysterious personage by whom Hitler was to be sealed of the children of Lucifer did not fail to make his advent at the appropriate time.

In the year 1919 the great south German city of Munich was perhaps the maddest spot on the map of Europe. Germany, defeated, yet smouldering, was in a mood of suppressed fury. All the wild wits of the Reich seem to have gathered in the hysterical capital of Bavaria. The Government of the new German Republic, to ensure itself against the many conspiracies which were directed against it, appointed so-called ' inspectors ' to report upon the activities of the numerous agitators who infested the seething capital of Bavaria. These were virtually its spies, its informers. Among them was Adolf Hitler, the ex-corporal of Bavarian infantry. It was his business to know and suspect everybody, and he soon found himself investigating the bona-fides of one Alfred Rosenberg, a bilious and disgruntled but eloquent refugee from Tallin, or Reval, in Estonia, to whom he had been introduced by Dietrich Eckart, an enthusiastic nationalist poet.

When the secret history of these dark and menacing times is at last unveiled in its entirety, one name will stand out upon its vexed pages with almost the same threatening vividness as that of Adolf Hitler himself. It is that of the strange and sinister personality who lurks behind the stocky figure of the Führer as did Mephistopheles, the spirit of evil, behind the doomed Faustus of legend. Who is this man, Alfred Rosenberg, who seems to be almost unknown to the people of this country, who is seldom alluded to in the British Press, but who virtually dominates the mentality of the German Reich as the director of its Culture ? For twenty-one years he has acted as the second self of the Führer, prompting his fantastic policy, inciting him to the wildest frenzies of race-hatred, and, above all, urging him continually to the destruction of the Christian faith in Germany.

Who is this ill-omened and secret man, who, even in

Nazi circles, is variously known as 'the best-hated man in Germany,' 'the German Antichrist' and 'the devil's advocate'? How did this Baltic German from Reval, this bitter and jaundiced propagandist with the mysterious past, brimming with violent hate against the Christian faith, succeed in gaining the whole-hearted confidence of an egoist so jealous and suspicious as Adolf Hitler? Feared and detested even by Goering and Ribbentrop, he has the ear of the Führer at times when even they cannot penetrate to the presence. These questions I shall try to answer as they should be answered.

At his first meetings with Rosenberg, Inspector Hitler found himself up against a human enigma. Rosenberg, he discovered, had been rejected as a volunteer officer by the Czarist military authorities, and was a stout opponent of the Kerensky and Soviet parties. Previously to the outbreak of war, he had been an architectural student, like Hitler himself. But behind all that was a period of vague and unsatisfactory mystery for which nobody could account.

When he tried to draw this sphinx-like refugee into conversation, however, Hitler speedily felt his doubts taking wing, for Rosenberg's political and nationalist views were practically the reflection of his own. The only difference between the general attitude of the two men to affairs political, was that while Hitler had not yet made up his mind concerning the appropriate treatment of Germany's problems, and, owing to his faulty education, had large gaps in his knowledge of history and economics, Rosenberg seemed to be master of a Germanic policy complete in every detail, and was deeply versed in German history, especially that part of it which had a bearing on the subject of Pan-Germanism.

His dearest topic of conversation was the moral grandeur and mental superiority of the German race, and the glorious destiny, in due time, would bestow upon it the suzerainty of the world. Day after day the enthusiastic and receptive, yet comparatively ignorant, soldier listened with rapt attention while the erudite and well-informed Russo-German theorist poured into his enchanted ears his fiery gospel of Nordic supremacy.

If the races of Europe were to be brought eventually under the beneficent rule of the just and enlightened German mind, said Rosenberg, it would first be necessary to destroy Christianity with its timid and outmoded notions of pity and kindness. After all, the Christian gospel was merely a Jewish imposition, a fraudulent conspiracy of the weak and cunning Semite to rob masculine and intellectual society of its birthright. But, so that the German race might have a spiritual background, it must be given a new faith to inspire it. The old war-like region of Odin and Thor, the cult of her fighting ancestors, must be restored to Germany—by degrees, of course, so that the people might be gradually weaned from their effete 'Nazarene' doctrines. On that, indeed, Rosenberg insisted even more than upon the racial theories which so deeply obsessed his hearer.

Before twelve months had passed Adolf Hitler had whole-heartedly accepted the views of the eloquent and mysterious refugee as completing and justifying his own more nebulous ideals. The pair were inseparable, and when, some years later, the Nazi Party became sufficiently powerful to put forward its programme and had funds at its disposal, Hitler appointed Rosenberg Director of its Foreign Press propaganda and made him editor of the *Völkische Beobachter*, the leading Nazi newspaper. When at last a Nazi Government was formed, he appointed his familiar as its Minister of Culture for the Reich and later as its Foreign Minister.

As we shall see, Rosenberg made full use of his position to carry out a programme bitterly hostile to the Christian faith. He urged Hitler to force upon the Churches, both Protestant and Catholic, the acceptance of a novel religious ideal which he described as 'Improved' or 'Positive' Christianity. This innovation was of a nature so revolutionary and unorthodox that it naturally aroused widespread opposition. Hitler, now Chancellor, agreed with its provisions, but suggested caution in the application of the new proposals, as he was fearful of arousing popular indignation at a critical juncture in the Nazi Party's affairs. But, as we shall see, the 'Director of Culture' exceeded his orders and practically took matters into his own hands. With fanatical zeal, he published a blasphemous book, *The Mythus of the Twentieth Century*, in which, while purporting to outline the new dispensation, he gushed out all the pent-up fury of his hate against Christianity, denying the Christian God, asserting that the Saviour was 'a Nordic revolutionary of stern purpose—a Hitler-figure,' whose teaching had been garbled and abused by later Jewish writers, and generally employing that kind of argument which from the first has been recognized as belonging to the technique of one kind of authority only—the common enemy of God and mankind.

Hundreds of Lutheran pastors dissented from his wild and impious doctrines. These, by the aid of the Gestapo, he banished to concentration camps, where they were treated with particular brutality. He forbade the use of the Cross as a symbol, expunged the name of the Trinity from the Church services, and introduced a form of Communion in which the congregations were taught that the Sacrament was 'the story of bread,' which told them 'how wheat had died to become bread, so that man might live.'

Blasphemous hymns were written for the use of the new Nordic Church, pagan festivals were celebrated by the notorious Jew-baiter Streicher on the Hesselberg mountain, and the 'black-coat swindle,' as Rosenberg called it, was impeached in a tireless propaganda.

It is known that Hitler received the greater part of his racial philosophy from Alfred Rosenberg. Those ideas which were loosely floating about the Führer's brain in an inchoate way before he met Rosenberg, were systematized by this well-grounded colleague. Rosenberg is not a Jew, as many people have concluded from his name, which is a perfectly good German one, but very definitely a Teuton of Baltic descent, whose training and preferences have given him a 'White Russian' outlook.

He has been called 'the most unpleasant personality in Germany.' Scores of powerful people dislike him cordially. His chief enemy seems to be Field-Marshal Goering, who appears to be suspicious of his murky past, according to some reported conversations. He is the chief protagonist of the eastward expansion of Germany, the plan underlying which is to attack Russia, subdue her, and seize upon the Balkans. But his grand obsession is said to be an anti-Bolshevist one. His private bodyguard is composed of Russian aristocrats, and he is a consistent opponent of a policy of *rapprochement* between Germany and Russia.

A good many questions have been asked in Germany as to the manner in which Rosenberg occupied his time between the commencement of the Russian Revolution and his appearance in Munich in 1919. Absolute mystery surrounds this passage in his life, nor has he ever sought to dissipate that mystery. But some of this uncertainty regarding Rosenberg and his background may be dispelled by an examination of his published writings.

The most outstanding among these is his book *The Mythus of the Twentieth Century*, published in 1930, and if anything were required to demonstrate, more than has already been done, the profane and anti-human character of this man, it is to be found in the pages of this prolix and gusty performance, which has achieved a circulation in Germany second only to the Führer's *Mein Kampf* itself.

This blatant and characteristically crude and violent polemic, the seven hundred pages of which bear all the ear-marks of diabolic anti-social fury, is divided into three sections, the first part expounding the 'myth' of the new religion of Nazism, which is the worship of race, while the second outlines the character of the novel faith itself, and the third surveys the international implications which arise out of these socio-religious doctrines. It may be said at once that, so far as the political part of it is concerned, it merely echoes and ratifies the general conclusions of the Pan-German school of writers, of which it is an imaginative expansion, without adding or subtracting any considerations of cardinal importance.

From the first, however, Rosenberg strikes an anti-religious note. The book, he tells us, is intended for all those Germans who 'have lost their spiritual contact' with either the Lutheran or the Roman Catholic Church. Life and history, he says, are beginning to take on new values. Class and religious oppositions in human society are no longer important or significant. The element which really matters is that of race. ' Soul ' means ' race,' for race is the outer form of the soul. (34.)

Humanity and the Church no longer represent absolute values. They are mere abstractions. The law of the blood alone determines, and must henceforward determine, the ideas and actions of men. The man detached from the ties of blood falls an easy victim to abstractions. Admixture with alien blood is of the nature of incest and spells death to race and civilization. (35.) The absurd paradox into which Rosenberg has fallen here will be manifest to everyone.

The Germanic race is the race *par excellence*, humanity triumphant. ' It has been a truism for a long time that all the Western States and their creative values have been produced by the Germans.' (36.) But Germany must rise to ' an ennobled achievement ' by a purification of her ancient blood, or be absorbed in the polluted human masses of ' the cosmopolitan cities.' The outstanding German virtues, everyone will be glad to hear, are heroism and honour. From honour springs freedom. But freedom, it must be understood, is for the German race alone and not for ' dark hybrids ' such as Czechs, Poles, and Levantines. And honour is only a vital power in a nation which has control of sufficient living space. As territorial dominion shrinks, so does honour.

Here we may glance at the third section of Dr. Rosenberg's book, that which deals with world history and Internationalism, as being in consonance with its first part. The idea of Internationalism, above all things, must be extirpated from the German mentality. The several agencies which have so far contributed to Internationalism are Freemasonry, Jewry, and Proletarianism. Freemasonry and its propaganda, he assures us, is the source of all false notions of liberty and, therefore, of racial decay. Owing to this outrageous and ' egotistical gospel of individual happiness,' the fundamentals of Germanism were undermined. Any Jew, Negro, or Mulatto could become a European citizen with full rights. To this monstrous insult to the purity of race was added another and still more degraded notion, the result of a foolish pity. (37.) European States were filled with luxurious asylums for incurables and lunatics. Wherefore should this *canaille* of the maimed and mentally alienated flourish in a continent intended by Providence for the maintenance of warriors ?

Having delivered himself of these charmingly humanitarian sentiments, Rosenberg proceeds to deal with his *bête noire*, the Jew. The Jew is, of course, the chief miscreant, the arch-plotter against the purity of race and the prime disseminator of a false literature. Through his capitalistic ideals he aims at world-domination. But it is unnecessary to deal at any length with the Nazi doctrine of anti-Semitism, which is written in the blood of its unhappy victims across the map of a distracted Europe.

Of proletarian hopes Rosenberg would make short work. These are ' brutal and infamous conceptions,' fulfilled with the absurd notions of sacrifice and love, which have insulted ' blood ' and ' honour ' past endurance by their absurd demands for better social conditions. National Socialism, which is the safeguarding of the State and the protection of its racial strength, is the one type of Socialism worth maintaining. (38.)

A coalition of European States can exist only under the leadership of the Nordic nations. France has become ' the deploying ground of Africa,' and is no longer a European State. Russia must be so confined as to remove its centre of gravity to Asia, where it belongs. Britain will become an outpost of the Nordic State in the West, to safeguard German interests on the Atlantic.

Throughout these pages one encounters again and again the Pan-German cry of the ineffable superiority of the Teutonic race, from which all progress and civilization emanates. From Germany has sprung the seed of all civilizations, Indian, Persian, Greek, and even Palestinian, the strength of the Roman Empire, the British power, the

French, the Syrian. But we have all retrograded. We must return to the early Teutonic simplicities. Christianity has destroyed us. It has been a disaster, the most fell in the world's history. So far as it is a good and beneficent force, it has drawn its sole virtues from the German character alone. Those German qualities ' are eternal and everything must be subordinated to them,' and those who do not agree with this view ' must not be spared.'

And then, in the full frenzy of his diabolic spleen, Rosenberg launches forth upon his grand diatribe against the Christian faith. The rancorous antipathy which Dr. Rosenberg and his disciples display toward Christian institutions cannot but be regarded as a part of the proof that their endeavours are fundamentally hostile to the whole spirit and tradition of Christianity. Nothing, surely, could be more strikingly inconsistent than that a system, which claims to receive its initial impulse from Christian tradition, should reveal so profound a dislike and contempt for the source it pretends to acknowledge as the basis of a new and superior dispensation. This supercilious and sometimes malignant disdain for Christianity is, indeed, its most salient characteristic.

It is proverbial that where this insensate hate for Christianity is found Satanism is to be suspected. The Freethinker may disagree with the tenets of Christianity, but he does not usually condemn it, and very frequently applauds it is a force for good, taking exception to its dogma only. But the Satanist, or ' Palladian,' cannot speak or write of the Faith without revealing a malevolent antipathy.

But, I would indicate a still more definite point of contact between the doctrines of this man and those of the Luciferian school. Like other students of the arcane, I have from time to time had access to unpublished documents formerly belonging to certain Luciferian bodies in France and elsewhere, some of which are now happily disbanded. For the most part, these are kept as curiosities by well-to-do collectors of occult literature and shown only to the favoured few, but others, such as the collection of the Marquis de Paulmy, are to be found in such Con-

tinental libraries as the Bibliothèque de l'Arsenal in Paris.
I am thus in a position to say that Dr. Rosenberg's essay,
or that part of it which deals with the ' reconstruction '
of German Christianity, contains so many of the arguments
and even the phrases to be encountered in Satanic manuscript literature as to leave no doubt whatsoever of the
source whence it emanates. It springs, indeed, from the
same poisoned wells as the Fourth Book of *The Occult
Philosophy* (attributed to Agrippa, but certainly without
valid authority, as it has little in common with the rest of
his works), with *The Elements of Magic*, by Peter D'Apono,
and *The Great Conjuration*, also in the Arsenal Library
at Paris. The entire spirit which pervades Rosenberg's
audacious and blasphemous work is faithfully transferred
from the manuscript pages of the lucubrations of the
Palladist schools, in fact, in many places I have found
that the words and phrases he employs are mere trans-
lations from French and Italian Palladist manuscripts,
transferences from some Luciferian scripts which probably found their way to his native Reval, the Baltic States
being notoriously the chief arena of the darker occult
sciences during the last two centuries.

But even stronger evidence that Rosenberg drew his
scheme for a new Germanic faith from Luciferian sources
is forthcoming. It is to be found in his pretension that
this new dispensation is not destructive of Christianity
but rather reconstructive of it. For that is the favourite
Satanist mode of attacking Christian dogma, and has been
so for ages. It is, indeed, that which from the first has been
suggested to the destroying agent by the inner councils
of Luciferianism as not only the most damaging, but that
which is also the most likely of success.

It is here, too, that the impudent and impious folly
typical of the Satanist, becomes apparent. Dr. Rosenberg
—woe worth the university which conferred its degree
upon him !—must indeed have suffered from that despic-
able form of credulity which is the mental caste-mark of
the diabolist when he penned his infatuated treatise. Did
it never occur to him that someone who had examined
the available manuscripts of his cult out of literary curiosity

might not sooner or later unmask the nature of his sources and reveal the true tendency of his monstrous purpose? The average German theologian (and, it is evident, many British and American theologians who have criticized his scheme) probably knows nothing of arcane literature on its darker side, no more, perhaps, than he does of natural religion or mythology, or the miserable origin of this anti-christian conspiracy would long ago have been revealed.

Those who know the paths which lead to such writings as the manuscripts of which I speak will require no further proof of their existence, and it lies upon them and upon the owners of those scripts to justify the truth of what I say. But that they should not be released for publication or general perusal is one of the common tenets of that code of decorum which Dr. Rosenberg and his coadjutors have done their best to break down. It is, indeed, notorious that this destructive and abhorrent literature of the pit has an effect of seductive glamour upon the weak-minded and the unwary which constitutes the best reason why the caskets which contain it should remain unlocked.

But it is time to inquire what precise use Dr. Rosenberg and his school have made of these sources. With uncouth precipitation, he repudiates the Creator and substitutes for Him a man-made deity, the personification of his own desire. Who is this ' god ' ? He is the deification of the German race. The Teutonic Narcissus looks upon the surface of the dark pool of his own spirit and beholds therein the reflection of a mighty warrior—himself.

For there are two forms of Christianity, we are told, the positive and the negative. (39.) The negative is that of ' the Syrian-Etruscan, or Jewish tradition,' ' a tradition of abstract doctrines and ancient rites,' while the positive Christian attitude ' awakens once more the power of the Nordic blood,' and its doctrines are framed in accordance with German proclivities and ideals. The Roman and Protestant Churches ' stand in the way of the vital powers of the Nordic race, and they must yield place. They will have to be transformed into a Germanic Christian faith.' These Churches declare that faith determines man. On the contrary, says Rosenberg, it is man who determines faith. (40.)

The sense of sin, he continues, is a mythical quantity, a mere Christian invention, ' which always goes hand-in-hand with physical and racial cross-breeding.' A Christianity which attempts to establish one standard of faith for Nordics, Negroes, and Levantines alike, is unthinkable. The dogmas of love and pity, so prominent in Christianity, merely protect ' all things and beings inferior, ill, crippled, maimed and rotten. . . . A notion which worshipped honour and duty would not preserve decadents and criminals, but would eliminate them.'

Rosenberg's ' Positive Christianity ' is ostensibly a modern form of Christianity specially adapted to the peculiar needs and circumstances of the Germanic race. That it is nothing of the kind, but that it has been designed with maladroit cunning as a temporary phase or ' evolutionary form,' intended for the gradual alienation of the German people from orthodox Christianity and leading to the eventual establishment of a primitive Teutonic mythology of the crudest form, is now abundantly clear, not only from the more recent writings of a host of propagandists, but also from the well-authenticated examples of pagan ritual which its debased worship affords, and its educational propaganda inculcates, as well as from the fiery infidelism of its more forthright apologists.

So far Dr. Rosenberg's unmeasured hatred of the Godhead has not been illustrated In the following chapter we shall see to what depths of infamy it permits him to descend.

CHAPTER VII

THE NAZI PAGAN CHURCH

IT is when he approaches the question of the existence of God that Rosenberg reveals the true *furor* which denotes the Satanist. " This demon of the desert ! " he shrieks. " This demon raised to a god," " this god-tyrant." (41.) Are these expressions not reminiscent of

the blasphemous outbursts of the Marquis de Sade, or the
'anti-God' propaganda of the early Bolshevists, when, in
the columns of the *Bezboznik* newspaper the cry was
raised : 'This year we must have new victories over the
hideous spectre of God'?   Many will also recall that the
Pravda flaunted the heading : 'War on the Denizens of
Heaven !'

But Rosenberg's wrath differs in kind from that of the
Bolshevists, for, whereas they made no pretensions to
anything but a downright atheism, he claims to be a
Christian man desirous of refashioning the Christian faith
to his own pattern and plan.   That is, he wishes to reform
it, much as did Martin Luther.   But did Luther hurl
blasphemies against God, did he trample on the Cross, did
he introduce a nauseous paganism into the body of his
Protestantism ?

The Satanist is not content with ignoring religion, or
spreading propaganda to its detriment.   He must also
insult its symbols and trample upon its gospels.   Thus,
to Rosenberg, the Old Testament is a mere reminiscence
of Jewish superstition, in which 'stories of cattle-drovers
and exploiters of prostitutes' are the central figures.   For
these there must be substituted 'the Nordic sagas and
fairy-tales.'

And if we ask who or what is to replace God the Father
in the Nazi religion, we are told that the adoration of the
people is to be directed toward the figure of the German
warrior, the shining Siegfried-hero of the ancient sagas.
But not impersonalized.   Rather does he assume the
shape and aspect of Adolf Hitler himself.   This is not
only the plainest matter of fact, but is, indeed, notorious.
'The simple, believing Nazi soul,' writes Sir Charles Grant
Robertson, Vice-Chancellor of Birmingham University, in
a striking pamphlet (42), 'speaks of him as "Saviour,"
"sent from God," "our Christ".'   This popular desire
for the Führer's apotheosis is also recognized by Dr. George
Norlin, President of the University of Colorado, who, in
criticizing the German Pagan Movement, writes of Hitler :
'He has become the Messiah, he has become the way, the
truth and the light.' (43.)

Dr. Ley, a prominent Nazi State Minister and leader of the Labour Front, makes this abundantly clear in his *Schulungsbrief*, a letter of instruction to educational authorities. 'We believe,' he writes, 'in this world on Adolf Hitler alone. We believe that the Lord has sent us Adolf Hitler, that Germany should be established for all eternity.' In many a house and public place in Germany, according to competent observers, shrines to Hitler are set up in prominent positions, where his portrait is illuminated by candles and wreathed with floral tributes.

Perhaps one of the worst of Nazi crimes is lack of humour. As a leader, Adolf Hitler is incredible enough to most non-German people. But as a 'god,' he cuts a poor figure, even beside the 'Black-fellow' deity Daramulun, or the Aztec Uitzilopochtli, neither of whom are notable for personal attractions.

Nor does the blatant impiety of Nazi intention cease here. Adolf Hitler is to become not only the Allah of the new faith, but its Mohammed as well. He is to recast, rewrite, the New Testament in such a manner that it will become acceptable to the Nordic outlook. German humanity, we are told, awaits the appearance of a fifth gospel—a gospel not inspired or dictated by God, as was that of the old dispensation, but by 'one man, who longs as deeply for its purification as he has studied it scientifically.' (44.)

This is, of course, the chiefest ambition of the veridical Satanist, of the false Messiah—to pose as a God and to garble the Scriptures. The dark powers and their ministers cannot resist the temptation to tamper with the Bible, to deface and outrage it. The pages of the history of Infidelity are littered with instances where the pseudo-god, inspired by Lucifer, instead of erecting a religion as of new, and of his own volition, has preferred to seize upon the attributes of God or of His Son, and to maim and wound His Word according to his own pestilent imaginings. Truly, as has been said, 'Satan is the ape of God.'

Along with the Scriptures, the symbols of Christianity must be cast into the fires of Wotan. The Cross, 'the symbol of death,' must be ruthlessly eliminated. (45.)

It must be replaced by the swastika. This emblem, which, we are told, was expressly adopted by Adolf Hitler himself, as the badge of his afflicted party, is not only a most ancient pagan device, but is well known as a Satanist symbol—'the broken cross,' typifying, as it does, the Christian cross defaced. Its earliest form seems to have been what is known to students of Comparative Religion as a 'compass-direction,' pointing, as it does, like a sign at four cross-roads, to the points of the compass, the quarters of the earth, whence proceeded the influences of the gods which governed these quarters. It is, in this sense, the symbol of the blood-stained deities of ancient Mexico, and it is the cross upon which the Hindu All-father crucified his son, Surya, lord of the sun. It is certainly associated in ancient Masonry with the idea of human sacrifice to ensure safety to a building. (46). Other authorities derive it from an early symbol of the primordial ocean-chaos, whence arose the earth and the heathen deities of many mythologies, while still others believe it to be the 'Mill' which agitated that primordial waste of waters, as in the Hindu myth of the 'Churning of the Ocean.' But it is unquestionably to be found in numerous *grimoires* and magical books of the more demonic kind.

Along with the man-god, Adolf Hitler, the pagan Nazis have placed as a goddess the figure of the German mother-soul. Rosenberg's henchman, Professor Bergmann of Leipsic University, evokes from the shades of Valhalla the abundant maternal figure of Frau Hölle, disguised as the mother-soul of the German race. ' In the German Church,' he says, ' there must be, along with the man-heroic figure, the beloved and faithful picture of the most blessed Mother, if the Church is to rest on the laws of life of a people's Church.' After the politic manner of the modern German religious apologist he refrains from giving the mother-goddess her native appellation as the great subterranean deity of old Germany and patroness of the witches, and blasphemously associates her with the Virgin Mary, a stratagem which will by no means commend itself to the sorely tried Roman Catholics of Germany. ' Many of our

Catholic comrades,' he suggests, 'will find it easier to accept the German national religion when they find the smile of the God-mother in the new German Cathedral '— a statement which not only reveals the purpose of this clumsy and blasphemous artifice, but which is at once a grave offence to loyal Catholic sentiment and to universal Christian piety. (47.)

But let us probe more deeply into the ' philosophy ' of Nazi paganism as represented by the writings of its foremost apologists. One of these, Dr. Wilhelm Kusserow of Berlin, Vice-President of the Nordic Faith Movement, deals quite openly with the origin and motive powers of the universe in a spirit of the grossest pantheism. Within the universe, he tells us in his *Das Noreische Artbekenntnis*, there exist ' forces or powers which we perceive as either doing or creating, or undoing and destroying.' As regards what is outwith the universe, we must not waste our time. Nothing exists there. The universe is without beginning or end, so far as man is concerned, and it is bootless for him to vex his understanding in speculating upon its origin. Christianity believes in eternal peace ; Nordic man in eternal struggle. (48.)

This gives us a clue to the materialistic basis of the Nazi faith. But it requires an apologist such as Dr. Rosenberg himself to indicate the manner in which this pagan farrago is to be amalgamated with Christian ideals. Dealing with the personality of Christ, he lays it down that He was ' of Nordic origin,' a reformer, a stern ' Hitler-figure,' whose history and beliefs have been rendered unrecognized by Christian apologists and propagandists.

These, he insists, were mostly Jews or Syrians, politically and spiritually in a condition of decadence. Animated by the spirit of revolt, ' Jewish fanatics ' like Matthew, Paul, Tertullian, pandered to the lower orders and riff-raff, first of the Syrian cities, then of Rome, announcing a gospel of love and pity which glorified the debased and gave only a secondary and passing significance to ' that code of honour so dear to the Nordic mind.' Their aim was, of course, to bring about the rule of Jewry, and in doing so, they dealt an almost irreparable blow to Nordic ideals and to the soul of Northern Europe, with its traditions of ' manly heroism.' (49.)

These strictures upon the tradition of the Christian faith go far to establish the real character of the Nazi departure as not only out of all sympathy with orthodox Christianity, but as deliberately hostile to it. When we read that the new Church will be joined ' only by those of Nordic descent,' its racially exclusive character, an attitude which definitely dissociates it from Christian tradition, becomes baldly apparent. But one detects an even more fundamental vein of animosity and pagan sentiment in the statement that Christianity on its first appearance in Europe deliberately wrecked ' the religious genius ' of the Nordic spirit by the introduction of alien forms subversive of its ' later mythological epoch '—that is the period when native Nordic beliefs were struggling towards a more complete expression. With equal justice it might be claimed that Christianity overthrew the groves of Druidism and put an end to the cannibal orgies of Polynesia.

The shallow and impious pretence that the new cult is rooted in a genuine and ' non-Jewish ' view of pre-Scriptural Christianity is readily disposed of when the arguments which describe its adaptation to the German temperament and ideals are closely and faithfully examined. It is demonstrable not only that such slight and partial adherences to Christian doctrine as ' Positive Christianity ' originally revealed were at a later stage rejected or still more grievously distorted, but that even from the first the whole genius and indwelling spirit of mercy and benevolence characteristic of the Christian faith have been perverted and misconstrued with a violence and contempt for its principles which argues that the cynical innovators of the new dispensation regard the adoption of any part of these as merely in the nature of a temporary stratagem designed to placate orthodox opinion in Germany and elsewhere.

As in her political attitude to the outer world, so in her religious policy, Nazi Germany speaks with the ambiguous utterance of Delphic oracle. But within her own confines she cannot refrain from victorious recitals of her disinge-

nuous methods in both of these spheres. What fresh complexion her novel religious code may have assumed since
the outbreak of war is unknown to the Gentile world, but
the likelihood is that a condition so favourable to its
gospel will scarcely have diminished its spread, although
it has been reported that the Bible is still a ' best-seller '
in Germany, its sales still considerably outnumbering those
of Herr Hitler's *Mein Kampf*.

A mystery of the blood is introduced into this already
involved faith, either to attract those of pseudo-mystical
tendency, or further to bowdlerize or ape Christian dogma.
By blood, by race alone, says Rosenberg, can the divine
nature of man be manifested, for ' Nordic ' blood repre-
sents that Mystery which has replaced and overcome the
old Sacraments.' In the peasants and workers of Germany
is still to be found ' the same myth-making power of
the Nordic soul as in the old Teutons who crossed the
Alps.'

I should like to make it clear that I am dealing in this
place especially with the proofs of diabolic and infidel
associations to be found in Nazi paganism and not so much
with what might be described (with rather grim courtesy)
as its ' theological ' pretensions, which have already been
criticized in half a hundred places easy of access to the
general reader, though, it must be admitted, with a surprising degree of delicate forbearance. Indeed, the absurd
theses advanced by its apologists are totally unworthy of
serious consideration. But for the elements of direct
denial we must seek not only in the writings of Dr. Rosenberg, but in those of his coadjutors.

Of these, Professor Ernst Bergmann of Leipsic is perhaps
the most downright. With Professor Bergmann there is
no beating about the bush. Bergmann is not a theologian,
but an art critic, yet his æsthetic solicitudes have not
restrained him from writing more than one book about
religion, his last and most serious effort in this respect
being his *Die 25 Thesen der Deutschreligion*—if the term
' serious ' may be applied to such a farrago of apostasy and
tribal cant.

In this book Professor Bergmann sounds a war-blast on

the pagan horn almost on the first page.   There are none of Rosenberg's earlier subtleties in his method.   'Away from Rome and Jerusalem!' he cries, 'Back to our native Berman Faith.'   'Our religion,' he continues, ' is no more that of the international Christ-God who could not stop Versailles.' (50.)   Christianity is 'an unhealthy and un-natural religion which arose two thousand years ago among sick, exhausted, and despairing men who had lost their belief in life.' (51.)   Still, Professor Bergmann, it built the greatest empire of faith the world has ever known—but that it may be 'unnatural' to the German Nazi tempera-ment one can well comprehend.

Yet, insists Bergmann, the two thousand years of Christian régime which Europe has experienced have been two thousand years of decadence and degeneration.   They have obliterated the German religion and culture which preceded Christianity, but which has now resurgently returned to its former place in German affections.   Ger-many needs a new religion frankly opposed to Christianity, which is alien to the German nature, 'because it is the creation of a pre-eminently Oriental mind. . . which con-tradicts at almost every point the German sense of custom and morality.'

And that, also, it is given one to understand !

The lack of natural cohesion brought about by this Eastern heresy has had tragic consequences for Germany in 'the suppression and repression of the native German religion, which, in the pre-Christian era had spiritually united the various German tribes.'   'The German religion is the form of faith appropriate to our age, which we Germans would have to-day if it had been granted to us to have our native German religion developed undisturbed to the present time.' (52.)

And Professor Bergmann revels in the name of 'heathen.'   He is not in the slightest degree disturbed by it.   'We who belong to the German religion are often called "heathens."   We reject this attribute if it refers to a religion belonging to a past age.   We do not, however, reject it if thereby is understood a religion free of Christianity.   In this case the word of insult, "German Heathen," takes on the aspect of a word of honour.   All the more, as to-day there is in Germany again a persecution of the Germans.' (53.)

These latter are perhaps the only words in Bergmann's book which hold any tincture of the truth.   There *is* a 'persecution of the Germans' in Germany to-day.   But who among the Germans are the persecuted and who the persecutors ?   The Nazi monsters, backed by the Gestapo, or the Lutherans and Catholics of Germany ?

But the new German religion is one of knowledge, not of faith.   'Like all Indo-Germanic religions, the German religion is one of knowledge rather than one of faith or of a dogmatic religion.   Odin, one of the noblest God-figures, was a God of knowledge.   He sacrificed an eye for knowledge, but not for an article of faith or a dogma.   A dogma is not worth a finger, not to speak of an eye.'

'Back to the forest' is the slogan of 'whole-hogging,' Professor Bergmann.   Back to the cult of the wild-wood, which latterly broke down into German witchcraft and Satanism, with all its murky abominations.   'We are no longer the ancient Germans.   That does not prevent us from entering deeply into the German forest-religion and from realizing that the Gothic dome is an imitation in stone of the Germanic holy forest-place and that Gothic in its entirety derives from the German soul.' (54.)

The idea of the fall of man is, to Bergmann, a theological myth and absurdity.   'So long as a man and the world are regarded as "fallen," such an experience (as is to be found in the Germanic religion) is not possible.   Everyone who seeks a pure religion and a pure life of God must keep himself painfully remote from the Bible and Christianity. *For there is a Satan in this religion.'*   So, with Luciferian adeptness the Professor turns their own batteries upon his opponents. (55.)

Correspondingly, the 'notion' of the immortality of man is abominable to the Professor.   'We therefore reject the belief in immortality and release as an offence to the Eternal Mother and as irreligious and immoral.   Such doctrines have nothing to do with religion. . . .   It is in spite of them and not because of them that many Christians are pious.'

E

A horrible and blasphemous picture is drawn of the Christ as a modern abortionist and 'Eugenist.' This is, perhaps, the basest vial of that poison which such men as Bergmann are pouring into the ears of youthful Nazis: 'If we wish to be Saviour, and this attribute is only possible for Man . . . we must take care that the sick and persons desiring release are not born. . . . This implies restraining the propagation of the inferior. . . . The day must come when Bethel and Bethseda will be in ruins and only healthy and happy men are there. . . . The best release we can find lies through service to people and Fatherland. . . . So the miserable little " I " is liberated. (56.) Pre-natal care, in the form of modern Eugenics, is the one right way to liberate Man. Christianity has stood in the way of this. Mankind, indeed, requires urgently to be free from Christianity and the Saviour " from beyond." . . . If Christ came back, He would be the first to reject this false picture which the Church has made of Him, and drive out the Church as firmly as he drove out the money-changers from the Temple. He would step down from the Cross, to which He is still nailed by false Christian conception, and become the modern doctor of the people and Eugenist, who releases men before they are born and not before they die. Such a Saviour is proposed by the German religion. We will no longer believe in Christ. We will be Christ ourselves and act as a Christ—among ourselves, our people, humanity.' (57.)

Lastly the whole doctrine of German paganism must be taught in the schools. 'We of the German Religion demand the introduction of religious instruction in the schools. Christian instruction can no longer be regarded as adequate or valid, since Christianity is in our sense no longer a religion.' (58.)

If these are not the demands of a self-confessed pagan and diabolist, how, indeed, are they to be described? Personally, I cannot find equations for them alien to associations which would infer a national back-sliding into a religion of devil-worship. It is as though an Oxford professor who was a member of the Church of England should go back to the mysteries of Stonehenge.

Let us make no mistake concerning this new 'German Christianity,' which, in some of its aspects, describes itself as *Neuheidnische Bewegung*, 'The New Heathen Movement,' which is led by callous apostles like Professor Wirth, J. von Leers, and Bernhard Kummer, and which purports to have 'an extensive international membership.'

One of its most subtle protagonists is Felix Fischer-Dodeleben, of the Monastery of Oliva, near Danzig. 'Wotan,' says Dodeleben, 'is nearer to us than the Christian God.' (59.) He claims that the personality of Jesus was distorted and misrepresented by early Christian apologists to serve their particular political and ecclesiastical purposes. 'In the Saxon book of Jesus, *Heliand*, as late as the ninth century, Jesus is represented as a stern Hitler-nature, who, without looking to right or left, pursues his high goal and rather goes under than seek safety by compromise.' (60.) The book *Heliand*, he refrains from adding, was a tract composed *ad hoc* to bolster up the blasphemous opinions promulgated by the Arian heresy, which denied the divinity of Christ, and has no official Christian authority behind it whatsoever. *Heliand* is most obviously the semi-pagan production of a dark age.

Dodeleben is also insistent that paganism be taught in the schools. The vanished world of the German past must be restored. 'To this period of the German-Nordic religion belongs also a careful study of how this Germanic world of Gods was conquered by invading Christianity. What concerns us is not the conversion and baptism stories which have been handed down to us, but the resistance offered by the Germans to their compulsory Christianization. Out of this resistance we can understand many of the habits and customs of our people—the very words of our present language, which otherwise are not to be understood. These things show how high was the religious culture of the Germans before it was destroyed. Names like Christmas, Easter, the weekdays and many others; the signs of runes, funeral practices, all require to be examined in this light. . . . They should form part of the religious lessons of our schools. They must become part of the instruction in all the organizations of the Party.' (61.)

This apostate father, like Bergmann, scoffs at the idea of immortality. 'Not only what is our spiritual abides when we are dead, but also our physical. For everything we possess in body and soul is inherited by our children from us, who thus make us immortal. There is no other immortality!' (62.)

The character and constitution of the new German 'Church' indeed furnish us with the best of proofs that the general movement which instigated it had its origin in influences of the most dubious description. Three separate groups or movements are capable of being distinguished, though all are united in a belief of the superiority of the German race and soul. Of these, ' the German Christians' were first in the field. Their creed may be described as a grotesque compromise with Christianity, and for some years they have exercised the most widespread authority and influence. To the harsh and unconscionable actions of the German Christians may be traced the persecution of the several German Lutheran Churches and their pastors, and for a time they certainly enjoyed the sinister support of the Gestapo in their ruinous and harassing campaign against established Protestantism, while they also employed the secret forces at their disposal to foment scandal and distraction in the Roman Catholic Church in Germany and Austria.

But the ' Nordic Faith Movement,' or the ' New Pagan Movement,' as it is known among genuine German Christians of both confessions, has of late revealed itself as an even more determined foe of the Christian faith. Founded in July 1933 by Professor Hauer, it adheres even more strictly to the doctrines of Rosenberg, while its dialectics assume a more ' philosophical ' and superficially logical complexion. It is also a mass movement of large popular acceptation, which the ' German Christian ' movement never was. In describing it, Dr. Wilhelm Kusserow, its Vice-President, states emphatically: ' That it assumes religious responsibility for the Nordic race ' and that 'its activities have to do exclusively with the Nordic faith and the national, moral, and religious attitudes which emanate from it.'

The Nordic Faith Movement, as regards those of its doctrines which deal with the origin and motive powers of the universe, reveals a marked materialistic tendency, although a pantheistic spirit also appears to infuse its ideas on occasion. But it is to the ritual as well as to the writings of the Nordic Faith Movement as a whole that we must turn for the fuller evidence of that definitely pagan attitude which presently inspires large numbers of Germans. These reveal that the movement has been powerfully influenced by the last and most ironically heretical and mischievous of those destructive forces which have agitated for the establishment of a new and specifically Teutonic dispensation—that which forthrightly and fanatically demands a complete return to Germanic paganism and the abolition of Christianity, as advocated by the late General Ludendorff, and which is still maintained by members of his family and a devoted circle of his warm admirers.

Persecution of the direst character has ever been the strongest weapon of the Satanist cult, and, as is well known, it has been a feature of the Nordic Faith Movement. Although Herr Hitler has, on several occasions, publicly announced that no victimization of any of the Christian sects in Germany would follow in the wake of the new régime (at the very time when persecution was most rampant), it proceeds with all the frenzied hatred characteristic of the Palladist tradition. Hundreds of Lutheran pastors in Germany have been cast into concentration camps, where they have been maltreated with the utmost ferocity because of their refusal to accept the blasphemous doctrines of the Nazi Church, whilst others have mysteriously 'disappeared' from their homes and charges. As 'the German Christians' now have complete control of the funds of the Lutheran Churches, it is competent for them to withhold his stipend and wherewithal from any pastor who does not absolutely and slavishly agree with their pagan outlook. To the honour of the

Lutheran ministry, be it said, large numbers have refused to adopt the novel dogmas—with results terrible to themselves and to their families. The dreaded Gestapo, which in this particular office has discovered a task peculiarly congenial to its dastardly ideals, not only drives these unfortunates from their incumbencies to starve, or to rot in the hells of the concentration camps, but dogs their unhappy families from place to place. Truly it may be said that in the devil-ridden Germany of to-day the blood of a thousand martyrs cries from the earth for vengeance upon their slayers.

The only comfort which an afflicted faith can accept from the present apparition of a devils' carnival in Germany is the certain knowledge of terrible retribution upon the miscreants who have brought this, as well as many another woe—woe heaped on woe—upon the body of a tormented Europe. That such retribution will follow, the whole testimony of history, the which is also prophecy, makes evident. 'God is not mocked.' Nor does He slumber, as the evil in their folly imagine. It is one thing to deny God but quite another to reckon with Him in the last event. Ripe is the red vineyard to the trampling of the grapes of wrath, and terrible indeed will be the vintage distilled therefrom !

A page, the most woeful in the history of mankind, has been written. Massacre in holocaust, servitude the most degrading, treachery unspeakable, persecution and cruelty scarcely to be named, have been crowded into one brief twelve-month of infernal orgy. The immediate miscreants will assuredly be brought to their assize. But what of the hidden, the concealed Cammorra, the Masked Ones, of whom they are but the creatures ? Are these once more to escape, as they did at the period of the French Revolution, at that of the Great War, at that of the Bolshevist outbreak, and on other countless occasions ? Are their sporadic but well-devised convulsions of hellish frenzy to continue to afflict humanity because its leaders choose to remain either blind to, or incredulous of, the existence on this planet of intelligences of a wickedness almost fabulous, guided and instigated by supernatural forces whose insane purpose is the extirpation of mankind ?

As I hope to make plain at a later stage, and, indeed, as I have more than once suggested in previous passages, the whole history of human tumult is eloquent of hidden agencies continually fomenting disturbance in the spheres of politics and international relationships. And, with most of the evidence before me, I refuse to believe that those activities are alone referable to the native wickedness of an unaided and unprompted caucus of 'gangsters.' No sane man or woman will for a moment credit that any other sane man, however normally depraved, could be so desperately inspired that, of his own volition, he would contrive abominations of such pitiless ferocity as the leaders of Nazi Germany have inflicted upon Europe. War he might well conceive. But to suggest that any normal person would precipitate such a Walpurgis Night of Satanic horror as the man Adolf Hitler has loosed upon a devoted Europe is in itself to brand him, and with him his colleagues as insane—and to impute to them a particular type of insanity, the insanity of demoniac ferocity—that which is known as 'possession.' For insanity is not necessarily homicidal nor blasphemous, nor do its victims usually co-operate, or comport themselves with the coldness of devilish malignity.

Nor have the brethren of the Catholic Church fared much better than those of the Lutheran. Their priests have been terrorized, their prelates assaulted by the Storm-troopers, their churches desecrated and their plate melted down. But Rome did not cower under these repeated insults. She placed Rosenberg's notorious book on the Index 'Expurgatorius,' uttering the well-merited rebuke that it 'rejected the very foundations of the Christian religion' and was designed to foster an ancient heathenism. The courageous sermons of Cardinal Faulhaber, Archbishop of Munich, on 'Judaism, Christianity, and Germany' shook the country to its base. Yet there was no man brave enough to protest, to align his own with the Cardinal's opinion. To do so meant the 'Siberia' of the concentration camps—a slow rotting of flesh and soul in a Gehenna of physical and spiritual torment. Again and again the late Pope pleaded with Nazi authority protesting that ' to set up a weird, impersonal fate against the living God ' was an act of profanity. His words might as well have been uttered to the frogs of the Pontine Marshes.

Let us now examine the cult and ritual of the German Pagan Church. The despair of the Lutheran Confessional Church at the doctrines and principles which are being imposed upon it is noticeable in a circular issued privately a month before the outbreak of war by its Provisional Council. In this agonized document the true character of the pagan notions underlying Nazi ' Positive Christianity ' are made plain enough. In the ceremony of baptism the name of the Trinity must no longer be mentioned. At confirmations children are made to swear that they will fight against Rome and Jewry. ' Both the Church authorities and the congregations know,' states the circular, ' that Communion is being celebrated as a festival of " blood and soil," or " as a symbol of the fact that bread was created by the death of wheat so that the world should be able to live." ' It is difficult to believe that this stark and crude symbolism from the ritual of the mysteries of Demeter of Eleusis should have found its reflection in a modern, European State nearly eighteen centuries after it was abandoned by the ancient world, or that the maladroit and ignorant interpretations of prentice myth-mongers should have been imposed upon a Christian congregation.

But the ' concentrated wheat ' need not be given to ' Nordic individuals,' who require no such pabulum, according to the Theological Congress of the German Churches at Weimar. Only ' individuals of the Eastern race,' psychologically speaking, of course—otherwise old-fashioned Christians and the young—need receive it ' as a sort of life-insurance ' or solatium. The cynical brutality of this utterance by men once ordained as ministers of the Lutheran Church, but now functioning as the officials of Nazi ' Positive Christianity,' is surely a terrible commentary on the change of spirit which has

overtaken the German race within less than a generation.
The desecration of the Sacraments is an age-old Luciferian
policy. Poignant, indeed, are those passages in the circular
in which the remnant of the faithful complain of 'the
struggle waged against the Old Testament, of the falsi-
fications of Biblical texts, and of the blasphemous utter-
ances which constantly occur in German Christian sermons.
(63.)

That these doctrines are reflected in a ritual of a naïve
and primitive kind is also glaringly apparent. 'We might
dismiss such a cult as fantastic,' writes the Rev. Henry
Sloane Coffin, President of the Union Theological Seminary
of New York, 'were it not for the horrible fact that this
faith is being shown in works.' (64.) As has already been
said, the Sacraments of the Confessional Church have been
cynically debased to the level of heathen allegory, or, as
Rosenberg has it, 'the mystery of the Nordic blood' has
'replaced and overcome the old Sacraments.' The hymns
sung at the meetings of the German Faith Movement are
eloquent of the pagan spirit which is rapidly breaking
through the veneer of Christian adherence.

> 'The time of the Cross has gone now,
> The Sun-wheel shall arise,
> And so, with God, we shall be free at last
> And give our people their honour back.'

That pagan ritual is indulged in is also on definite
record. At the Nordic Festival of the Summer Solstice
in 1938, and on the same occasion last year, the notorious
Julius Streicher, 'the Jew-baiter,' functioned as high
priest at an immense concourse on the Hesselberg, a
mountain declared sacred, by the Führer, on the slopes
of which great bale-fires were lit and mysterious ritual
acts performed. Rumours of animal sacrifice having taken
place on this occasion were hinted at by certain newspapers,
but these appear to have had no foundation in fact.
Standing before one of the bon-fires, Herr Streicher said:

"We need no men in black to whom to make our
confessions, that we may gain strength for the coming

E*

year. When we look into the flames of this holy fire and throw our sins into them, we can descend from this mountain with clean souls. We do not need priests and pastors. We have become our own priests. We approach nearer to God after climbing this mountain. Let people abroad criticize our worship as much as they like. The fact remains that God has always accompanied Germany on her way, even thousands of years before there were prophets or churches. The time will come when Germans will climb this sacred mountain not once a year but whenever they feel the need of worship which, formerly drove them into the churches. Be beautiful, god-like, and natural."

These bale-fires are 'restorations' from the ancient German fire-festival of the Sunnewende. Herbs are cast into the flames, to symbolize that with their burning all the troubles and vexations of the German folk will similarly vanish in smoke ! It is curious to'note, in the passing, that the name of the mountain on which this festival is held, the Hesselberg, which has been declared 'sacred' by Hitler, implies 'the witches' height' (hexe=witch). I lay no particular stress upon the matter, but it appears to me strange that Herr Hitler should go out of his way to select and 'sanctify' for 'religious' purposes a mountain formerly associated with the ancient witchcraft of Germany.

That the destruction of the Christian Churches in Germany has the fullest sanction of the Nazi Government is clear enough from a speech made by Dr. Alfred Rosenberg, at Nürnberg in 1938, when he said :

" That the Catholic Church and also the Confessional Church in their present form must disappear from the life of our People is my full conviction, and I believe I am entitled to say that this is also our Führer's viewpoint. . . . Furthermore, the development of our teaching scheme in schools of all categories is of such an anti-christian-Jewish type that the growing generation will be forewarned against the black-coat swindle."

In the Catholic Church, he added, there were 'sincere

Germans working as priests who could assist this longed-for development.'

That thousands of Germans, both Protestant and Catholic, detest the low-grade paganism which is being foisted upon them, and which now stands declared as a modern adaptation and development of the ancient Teutonic folk-religion outlined in Chapter III, is clear enough. In some districts, notable the Catholic Rhineland, the new doctrines and the interference to which they have given rise have aroused demonstrations of popular anger, the public meetings of the German Faith Movement have been broken up by the singing of hymns by mixed crowds of Protestants and Catholics, and attendances in the churches of both confessions have been greatly increased. In Dresden the former Crown Prince of Saxony, now a Catholic priest, has drawn large crowds to the Hof Kirche, and his sermons on such texts as ' Thou shalt have no other gods before me ' have been welcomed with such a degree of popular satisfaction and acclamation as to leave no doubt that large numbers of people in Germany fully realize and contemn the crassly pagan ideals which animate the founders of ' Positive Christianity.'

Perhaps the saddest feature of this breaking away from the Faith of centuries is the bedevilment of the minds of the youth of Germany. In the privately printed literature of the Nordic Faith Movement prepared for the instruction of the young, the ancient pantheism of Germany is lauded and rites and ceremonies are devised to take the place of Christmas and other Christian festivals. It is particularly impressed upon teachers that no hope of a life to come or any idea of salvation must be allowed to obtrude itself upon the child consciousness. ' We are fighting,' it is claimed in one of these publications, ' as our ancestors said, for the fashioning of the world by the side of the gods—that is, the German gods, not the God of an effete and outworn Christianity. It is urgently necessary that we should *all*, and especially the school youth, become well acquainted with the early Faith. Not that we may become worshippers of Wotan and Donar. . . . It is more serviceable for our people to occupy themselves with the beliefs of their own forefathers than with those of the Jewish people.

That this view proceeds from Hitler himself cannot be questioned. His alone must be the responsibility for poisoning the brains and souls of millions of young Germans by representing to them that the myths and sagas of their remote ancestors are not the relics of a past which they may study with curiosity and romantic interest, but rather the repositories of a heroic example to be closely imitated by them.

CHAPTER VIII

NAZISM AND SATANISM

NAZISM bears all the marks of that species of rule behind which the evil esoteric power conceals its distinctive purpose, a foul tyranny masquerading as a great popular movement of reorganization. We have seen much the same process in the case of Bolshevism, from which Nazism, as a system, differs not at all in kind, but in degree only. In short, Satanism in Germany is functioning through the Nazi régime as certainly as though the hidden directors of its cultus were housed in the departmental ' palaces ' at Berlin.

I have revealed—through the labours of others, as well as through my own—an exact ' genealogy ' and record of Satanic effort in Germany since the commencement of the Christian era at least. Beginning with the Satanist Bogomiles, a Manichæan sect, this descends through witchcraft and ' official ' Satanism to the Illuminati, and thence from them, through the Tugenbund and the Pan-Germanic societies, to the Nazi régime. The links are unbroken.

Even so, it is not necessary to prove the existence of a chain of secret diabolic effort descending through the centuries. Whatever its outward manifestations, the central nucleus of Luciferianism, its caucus, survives from age to age, handed down from hidden initiate to hidden initiate, a deathless lineage of evil. That existence is self-evident because of the unvarying nature of its results.

Nazism, indeed, reveals the self-same attributes and insignia as any other organization created under Luciferian auspices in the hellish and untiring cruelty which marks its treatment of its victims, in its hideous mendacity, which defaces the dignity of civilized humanity, and which recalls the savage faithlessness of a Central African potentate, or the brazen lying of the Oriental; in its insensate and homicidal hates and frenzies; in its ambition for mass slavery, serfdom, and forced labours; in the hideous immoralities which its private quarrels have revealed, which show some of its leaders to have been even beneath the brutes that perish in foul and abominable habitude; and in its flair for assassination.

All these symptoms have invariably manifested themselves on other occasions of revolution which are known and proved to have been inspired by Luciferian influence —in the French Revolution, in which the torch of conflagration was cast by the Illuminati, in the recent Spanish Civil War, which is known to have been planned by nihilist Satanist influence, in the Russian Revolution, when Bolshevism succeeded in gaining power in Russia, in the Mexican revolution. The list is, indeed, so long and so familiar that to quote from it further is merely to waste space in an hour of needful terseness.

Now in all these upheavals one outstanding circumstance is at once discernible—a hatred of Christianity, which immediately gluts its vengeance upon the Church and all that religion stands for. Had the revolutions I write of been actually of a 'social' character, had they sought to correct or abolish bad government or social abuses alone, their leaders would first have addressed themselves to the task for which they had ostensibly roused national opinion.

But what is the first and invariable result of their fury, that which displays the actual and underlying intention of those who originated them? It is the attack upon religion, the demonstration of a deathless hate against the Christian faith and all its works. In the French

Revolution they burned the churches and abbeys, massacred or banished the priesthood, and set up a Goddess of Reason and a pagan calendar. In Spain, as we have seen, the whole hatred of the Reds was let loose on the Church. In Russia the Bolshevists celebrated the 'death' of God, sacked the churches and abolished the Greek faith. In Germany the Nazis have now introduced a heathenism of their own manufacture. In Mexico the Roman Catholic Church has been disfranchised, and functions only on sufferance.

Are we to believe that the populations of these countries, their common people, acquiesced in these profanations, that the pious Spaniard and the no less devout Russian *mujik* at once cast aside the faiths of their fathers, that the Mexicans, so devoted to their priesthood, and the great mass of German Lutherans, so rightfully proud of the noble protest of their fathers under the great Martin Luther, all instantly conceived a contemptuous hatred of their several Christian confessions and resolved to adjure them and blaspheme them?

The bare notion is so utterly illogical as to confound itself. In all these instances the organization of revolt and sacrilege was in the hands of a comparatively small and compact caucus who exercised such complete command that the masses were utterly powerless to prevent them, and remained in silent terror and subjection, unless those of the rabble, who became the ready ministers of Satanist fury. Without the Illuminati there could have been no French Revolution. Had not the Bolshevist chiefs in exile been sent back to Russia in a special train by the German authorities, the revolution in that country, under Kerensky, would have taken on a milder, possibly a Liberal complexion. And had there been no Alfred Rosenberg, no General Ludendorff, there would certainly not have been any German Pagan 'Cathedral.' These insurrections and reversals of national life and policy were social in a secondary sense alone. Their prior intention, and the source whence they came, are visible in the insensate and blasphemous hate which one and all of them have revealed for the Christian faith. Their political aims and organization have been made the vehicle of Satanist purpose.

Before any man refuses to give credence to the appalling fact of a Satanist power functioning through revolution, he must put to himself certain questions : Why does violent popular unrest invariably manifest itself in a destructive way against official religion? Why does this hatred always take the self-same forms of the violation of Christian symbols, the distortion of the Christian gospels and the mockery of Christian rites, as though it followed a given tradition? Why, in all ages, have the official leaders of opinion invariably described these risings and movements as issuing from Satanist influence?

Are all the facts which I and other writers on this question have elicited regarding Luciferian influence and action throughout the centuries, to be set aside as mere inventions, or casual occurrences? Do they reveal nothing of definite and organized effort, from one generation to another? In acting as they have done, are not the Nazi authorities deliberately attempting to extirpate Christianity in Germany, precisely as did the Bolshevists in Russia, the native party in Mexico, or the Illuminati in the France of the eighteenth century? The arm of coincidence, long as it may be, is not sufficiently extensive to stretch across twenty centuries, nor to bridge so many geographical latitudes.

Germany, in the past, attempted to use the hidden forces of Luciferianism for her own behoof. The tables are turned. Satanism has yoked her to its chariot, has made her its palfrey. She has become the instrument of its lust and hate, as is proved by her thousand acts of demoniac ferocity, by her brazen mendacity, her enslavement of hapless millions.

In Bolshevist Russia, under Leon Trotsky, who has paid the penalty for his hideous crimes, Satanism ran riot. Disgusting parodies of Christian festivals and rites continually took place. These were generally ' celebrated ' outside some church, when a ' priest ' appeared in mock vestments and went through sham devotions. Finally, the choir sang well-known hymns, the altered words of which made mock of the Redeemer. (65.)

The Russian correspondent of the *Daily Herald*, writing on 24 January 1923, said : ' This is Sunday, and it is also the Russian Christmas Day (7 January). As far back as November last, the Bolshevists had determined to signalize it by a series of public antichristian processions. . . . The organization of these blasphemous orgies was left to the Komsomolov League of Youth, who . . . make a painful picture of demoralization, insolence, ignorance, filth, disease, and premature decay. . . . The procession took an hour to pass any given point. . . . The scoundrel who impersonated St. Joseph (?) was clearly of the lowest, most exaggerated, most repulsive type, and the hag who impersonated the Madonna and carried a dirty child in her arms was, I am told, a notorious prostitute. . . . One of the lorries . . . contained a group representing the Three Persons of the Holy Trinity, as well as St. Joseph and the Virgin Mary ; and every time the lorry halted this troupe went through a disgusting and indecent pantomime.'

In an account of a similar event, which appeared in the *Daily Graphic*, 18 October 1924, the writer says, a figure labelled ' Almighty God ' was burned in a bonfire, and adds : ' Not content with the abolition of God, the Bolshevists sought for further expression of their hatred of Christianity. They erected a statue to Judas Iscariot at Svishka, near Kazan in the summer of 1923, and the unveiling of this has been described by Halling Koehler, a Danish writer, who was present.'

The Nazi miscreants have not gone so far. But their blasphemies recall those of Bolshevist Moscow. They have tampered with the Sacraments, they have parodied the Gospels, they have mocked God the Creator, and have set up an idolatrous worship of Adolf Hitler in His place. Their sacrilege is only a degree less blatant. But that the spirit which inspires them emanates from the same source as that which inspired Bolshevist Russia to blasphemy is not to be questioned.

I have, in more passages than one, hinted at the existence of secret or hidden personages who are the real leaders of the Satanist power and who dictate its procedure and policy. That such leaders actually exist and have existed for centuries is clear enough from all the evidence. It will be recalled how Von Hundt, the emissary in Paris of Frederick the Great, when confronted with the falsehoods he had uttered concerning the countenance which Prince Charles Edward was alleged to have given to the Templar Order, in his confusion stated that he was directed in his actions from a hidden centre, and by 'Unknown Superiors,' whose identity he was bound not to reveal. (66.) 'The Rite of the Stricte Observance,' wrote the late Mr. A. E. Waite, 'was the first Masonic system which claimed to derive its authority from Unknown Superiors, irresponsible themselves, but claiming absolute jurisdiction and obedience without question.' (67.)

M. Copin Albancelli, to whose writings I have already alluded, mentions the existence of an inner circle in Continental Freemasonry, which he says is concealed and international in its character. This he calls 'invisible Freemasonry,' and says that it is recruited only from the groups of upper-degree Masonry, 'and perhaps, even in certain exceptional cases, outside these.' (68.) There is, he adds, 'a world existing behind the Masonic world, more secret than it, unsuspected by it as by the outside world,' and it is plain that Continental Freemasonry 'is more the dim antechamber of this actual secret society. 'There exists, then, of necessity,' he concludes, 'a permanent governing Power. That Power we cannot see, therefore it is occult.' Later, I am led to believe, M. Albancelli formed the view that the power in question was Satanic in its origin, and that it had brought about the Great War, but as I cannot trace these later writings I speak without due authority. As M. Albancelli was himself a French Freemason the value of his evidence is clear.

Galart de Montjoie, in his *Historie de Marie Antoinette* (1797—p. 156), speaks of the 'invisible hand which appears to have created all the events of our revolution,' while de Savine, in 1801, after the Revolution, alluded to 'an international sect . . . a power superior to all others . . . which has arms and eyes everywhere, and which governs Europe to-day.' De Malet, writing in 1817, declared that the Revolution 'forms a particular nation, which took birth and has increased in the dark amidst all civilized nations, with the object of subjecting them all to its domination.' (69.)

The German Freemason, Alban Stoltz, in a brochure published in 1862, says: 'There exists in Germany a secret society in Masonic form, which is controlled by unknown chiefs.' Even the Italian Carbonari were ignorant of the power which governed their diabolical fraternity.

Deschamps, who probably knew more about secret societies than any man, alluded to their hidden direction in his *Les Sociétés Secrètes et la Société*, in which he gave it as his opinion that it was not possible to discover whether there was any unity of direction among European secret associations in his day (he wrote in the seventies of last century) as the whole matter was most carefully concealed. At the same time, his researches led him to the conclusion that there existed 'a secret council which directs all Masonic societies,' and 'that there are secret lairs where the chiefs of the sects agree together on their work of destruction.' (70.) That the Bolshevist Revolution in Russia was brought about by secret leaders of whom the ostensible chiefs knew little or nothing has frequently been asserted by many writers.

As I have said, Adolf Hitler has a criminal record of such flagrancy that it seems rather to belong to a 'dark angel' than to a mere human being. Indeed, it is difficult to conceive of a modern white man revelling in such wholesale infamy, assassination, and unspeakable cruelty as he has done, reducing the neighbouring lands to helotage, flooding them in oceans of blood and bringing down an avalanche of flame upon peaceful millions, as might Lucifer himself, did the Powers of Heaven permit. Insane with vengeance for Germany's supposed wrongs he may be. But this, I repeat, is not the insanity of every day, it is something transcending the humanly irrational, it is demonic, gigantic, the hellish wrath of a spirit dominated by evil.

That this man's early acceptance of pagan ideas associated with ancient German tradition and legend has developed into a soul-complex I cannot doubt. As Adolf Hitler has

advanced in life there has steadily grown up within him
another man, rather an evil spirit, of the most violent
and deadly kind, to whose daily expansion he has offered
little or no resistance. In a word, the malign power has
seen in this base and pitiless creature, utterly lost to all
human sensibility, and moved only by crude and elementary
emotions of revenge and mock sentiment, precisely the
kind of vehicle which it sought, and which it ever seeks to
carry out its infernal purpose.

At the first, even the leaders of the Nazi Party themselves were dubious of Adolf Hitler, of his personality
and of the mystery which surrounded him. Heiden tells
us that a leaflet was circulated among its members de-
nouncing him in the most unmeasured terms, in which
his lust for power and personal ambition were stressed.
' He regards the time as ripe for bringing dissension and
schism into our ranks by means of *the shadowy people
behind him*,' runs the anathema of his colleagues. ' It
grows more and more clear that his purpose is simply to
use the National Socialist Party for his own immoral
purposes. A further point is the question of his occupation and finances. If ever individual members inquire
what he actually lives on and what his previous occupation
has been, he always gets excited and loses his temper. . . .
National Socialists ! Make up your own minds about such
characters ! . . . Hitler believes himself capable of leading
the German people astray.' (71.)

This document, issued by his own comrades, Streicher
among them, reveals the truth concerning Hitler's conduct of the Nazi Party in its early days and the damning
fact that he was himself the creature and instrument of
hidden forces which supplied him with the means of
wherewithal to carry out his work of interpenetration.
' The man,' says Heiden, ' is by nature secretive, his life
does not lie open to his friends. Questions regarding his
private affairs offend him.' (72.) He is awkward and ill
at ease in the company of superior men and frank outspoken
people, adds Heiden. He cannot face them, but rants and
storms, or relapses into a sullen moodiness.

That he is a man open to the promptings of the basest

and most absurd superstitions of a kind which no genuine mystic would entertain for a moment, is so notorious that I need only allude to it in passing That he is impelled by forces the true nature of which he does not comprehend, is plainly obvious from the account of those conversations he held with Sir Nevile Henderson before the outbreak of war, which makes it evident that he is under the domination of influences of which he is only the mouthpiece. His vacillation in arriving at conclusions is indeed, notorious. His mind and will are, in a word, at the mercy of that force which, thoroughout the ages, has masqueraded under many names, but which, nevertheless, has only one identity.

Adolf Hitler himself has told us that he is under the domination of a ' Voice ' which dictates to him his actions in all affairs of importance. " Unless," he says, " I have the inner incorruptible conviction : ' This is the solution,' I do nothing. But if the voice speaks, then I know the time has come to act." If the nature of this 'Voice' be judged by the acts it has dictated, it is surely anything but an angelic utterance.

Hitler's face, says Heiden, ' is a source of embarrassment to his followers, and of malicious joy to his opponents. . . . The Munich anthropologist, Von Gruber, has declared it to be racially inferior, and has given abundant reasons.' In the trenches, Heiden adds, Hitler's fellow-soldiers jeered at him as a ' lunatic.' Looked at full face, the countenance is the most commonplace imaginable, the face of a sullen lout, wolfish and truculent. Only in the eyes is a glimmer of something, difficult to define. But what that something is becomes clear enough, I think, when one sees the face in profile, especially when smiling. Then it is the face of a devil. ' How far Hitler's mind is a pathological problem remains for the present a secret among his doctors,' says Heiden. It is no secret, however, to the professional anthropologist, who has seen the faces or studied the photographs of low-grade savages, which, in repose, have the same expressionless appearance, and, when animated, wear the same fatal and homicidal leer.

Hitler's ' prophecies ' are typical of the Satanist dupe. Again and again false mystics have arisen in one country or another who succeeded in deluding the people for a season by uttering oracular predictions, doubtless received from those dark forces of which they were the creatures, for the purpose of arousing confusion and discord. No need to allude to them categorically. Their names suggest themselves at once. Such are the 'prophecies' of Adolf Hitler. The average medicine-man of a low-caste community could be relied upon to 'prophesy' with a greater approach to precision than does the German 'Colossus.' Nineteen years ago he predicted the speedy fall of the Soviet power. In 1923 he proclaimed that the French would never resign their hold on the Ruhr. While in jail he falsely foretold the triumph of his party at the polls in 1928. His predictions do not even bear the inferential double-meaning of the oracles of Dodona or of the Sybils. They are dictated by his Luciferian master, who is eternally incapable of speaking the truth because of that inability which is inherent in the Father of Lies—that extraordinary vein of stupidity which mercifully assails him when he gives utterance and which compels him to babble and stutter the inanities of a mendacity founded upon unreason and miserable pride. For all vices evil pride is the vice paramount. The acts of false pride, cruel as fire upon the foreheads of the humble, are perhaps the chief abominations of God. It is pride, the insurgent vice of Lucifer, which, mimicked by foolish men who have no ears for the voice of celestial wisdom, precipitates wars, transforms the friend into the enemy, which torches the fires of envy, and which abases many a man from natural nobility to the grade of the imbecile buffoon.

Here I may remark upon the seemingly contradictory circumstances that Hitler has expressed his deep suspicions of Freemasonry, which, he asserts, is the preserve of the conspiratorial Jew. But it may be observed that in his *Mein Kampf* his chief objection to this Semitic influence is its pacifist character, 'which paralysed the instinct for national self-preservation.' (73.) Rosenberg reveals an equal distrust of Continental Freemasonry, indeed all the Totalitarian Powers, Soviet Russia and Fascist Italy included, have banned Masonry from functioning in their

territories.   In reality, none of these Powers desires to be
the instrument and dupe of the evil forces.   Their more
responsible governors are perfectly well aware of the results
which arise from such an association, which makes for total
subjection to these over-riding influences, a tyranny of the
most abject character.   After all, they are governments,
corporate authorities, ambitious of full and undivided rules.
Among the first acts of the Soviet Republic was the extirpation of the Russian anarchists and nihilists, just as in
Italy the Fascist Government speedily disembarrassed
itself of all such rivalry as might be classed as revolutionary.
But in the protean spirit, which is racy of its genius for
adaptability, the Luciferian caucus has accommodated its
plans to fall in temporarily with systems which, in themselves, bear the poisonous germs of confusion, woe, and
chaos.   To their terrible master it matters not what complexion a party or a State may assume, or what its creed
may express, so long as these are inherently pernicious.
If it carries within it the seeds endemic to destruction and
human misery and misfortune, that is sufficient—the
Great Insanity is appeased and in the cunning which
inspires its madness, accepts the role of famulus, of a
ministering spirit, until such time as it may unmask itself
as arbiter and despot.

That is precisely what has happened in Germany.
Though the Nazi rule was intent on murder and violence,
and stern as was its grip upon a despondent people, an
almost miraculous order and discipline accomplished
numerous material works for their benefit.   A wise and
beneficent dispensation would have called for popular
co-operation and would have eschewed tyranny and persecution.   But the personal antipathies of the Führer for
the Jews and of his colleague Rosenberg for the Christian
faith, and the desire for territorial conquest, and, above
all, for revenge, gave the Powers of Evil their cue.   Fiercely
and promptly they acted upon it, and Nazi Germany, which
unpromising as were its beginnings, might gradually have
become a great and contented State and the leader of
European progress, relapsed into a hive of waspish myriads
ambitious only to overspread the lands of Europe and to

glut their vengeance on those whom they believed to be their hereditary enemies.

The Satanic power saw to it that Adolf Hitler was surrounded by colleagues affectionate to its ends, the most malign by far being its own selected emissary, Alfred Rosenberg, the Weishaupt of its revolutionary purpose. For if anything definitely marks this man as the evil genius of unhappy Germany, it is the manner in which he has striven to destroy her hereditary religious confessions. Equally significant is the fact that this measure proceeds from him and from him alone in the first instance, and that it was extraordinary to the general ideals of the Nazi Party and supererogatory to its impulses and intentions. Why, indeed, should it have been posed at all, if not for the reason that it was intended to carry out the behests of a power which had no interest in the Nazi programme otherwise than as an instument of discord ?

For it will not serve to argue that a return to the ancient faith of Germany was a plank in the original platform of the Nazi Party. It is perfectly true that the literature of Pan-Germanism, as expressed in the writings of Paul Lagarde and Houston Stewart Chamberlain, had advocated some such departure as an intellectualistic rather than a practical desideratum, but the rank and file of National Socialism were certainly not enamoured of it, and some of its leaders, particularly Goering and Goebbels, have never approved of it, nor of its prime apostle. Even Hitler himself, predisposed as he is to its thesis, at first alluded to it in the most wary manner imaginable. Of Rosenberg's *Mythus* Pastor Huffmeier, who was antagonistic to it, wrote : " The Party as such refused responsibility for the expression of religious views of one of its members, contained in the *Mythus*, however important the member might be. Naturally the demand for the book grew. Hitler's book was swallowed wholesale, but Rosenberg's book was also read by all those who made the least pretentions to intellectual development."

Again and again, Hitler protested that he had no intention of interfering with the religious life of the people of Germany, though he intended to regard ' Positive Christianity' as the basis of the State. He once said: " The National Socialist State is based on Positive Christianity. It will be my earnest effort to preserve the rights of both the great Christian Confessions; to defend their teachings against attacks and to establish their duties in harmony with the declarations and requirements of the established State."

On the day of Potsdam, 21 March 1933, he reiterated his intention to preserve the two great Christian confessions ' under the strong protection of the Reich and the State.' The programme of the Party demanded freedom for all religious opinions in the State.

But, later, Hitler unfolded his private opinions on the subject to Rauschning. He then said: " Fascism, if it likes, may come to terms with the Church. So shall I. Why not? That will not prevent me from tearing up Christianity root and branch and annihilating it in Germany . . . for our people it is decisive whether they acknowledge the Jewish Christ creed with its effeminate pity-ethics, or a strong heroic belief in God in nature, God in our own people, in our destiny, in our blood." Later, he said: " It's all the same old Jewish swindle. . . . A German Church, a German Christianity, is distortion. One is either a German or a Christian. You cannot be both."

That Hitler's mentality is under the influence of the Satanist power is evident from his vacillations, his lack of self-control, his epileptoid seizures of rage and the spirit in which he has dealt with the peoples of the neighbouring States which have fallen into his hands. Typically Satanist, also, is the manner in which his campaigns have been conducted, the treachery and perfidy which have been features of them disclosing time-honoured Satanist stratagems and methods.

As regards Alfred Rosenberg, his Mephistopheles, he is, as Heiden puts it, ' a German by descent, but a Russian in mentality.' He appears to have been educated first in Riga, then in Moscow. For a time he was an instructor in draughtsmanship in Russia. Then, as one writer remarks, ' a period of mystery followed.'

We must remember that this man was German Minister for Foreign Affairs during the most delicate period in international relations between Nazi Germany and the outside world, that he has been Hitler's *alter ego*, ever at his elbow, prompting, instigating. But he possessed the confidence of no one else. Large sections of people in Germany dislike Rosenberg intensely, indeed detest him. The popular nicknames bestowed upon him disclose how profound that dislike and distrust actually are—'The German Antichrist,' 'the devil's advocate,' 'the best-hated man in Germany,' 'the philosopher with the sour stomach.'

How closely this man resembles Adam Weishaupt, the Illuminatus, in his general method. He professes a respect for Christianity whilst labouring to destroy it ; he is careful to deprecate a policy of violence whilst actually carrying it out. Concerning his history no man knows anything definite.

My own impression is that this man is assuredly a Satanist emissary of high standing, as were Weishaupt, Clootz, and Michel Bakunin, closely in touch with the Luciferian nucleus, and cognisant of its actual directors ; that he was dispatched to Munich in 1919 for the express purpose of stirring up unrest in that distracted centre, that he saw in Hitler a tool wonderfully well adapted to his purpose, and that, by means familiar to Luciferian adepthood, he succeeded in placing Hitler under the spiritual control of those dark and fatal influences which dominate the Satanist caucus. For I believe that, just as God influences all things for good within the world, so does the Father of Evil, in base imitation of Him, seek to influence men for ill. That he has a commission so to do we know from Holy Writ, and to the man who does not credit this I would quote the words of W. E. Gladstone on the subject of disbelief in a Satanic power : "What is this but to emasculate all the sanctions of religion, and to give to wickedness, already under too feeble restraint, a new range of licence ?"

The Nazi directorate and, strangely enough, some of their fiercest opponents, have denounced the Jews as the protagonists of Black Magic in Europe. Here I do not intend to labour the point. The statement reveals itself as a typical Satanist invention. In the 'Kabbalah' the Jews possessed a corpus of literary mysticism which drew much of its content from ancient Babylonian sources. There is nothing whatsoever of Black Magic in the ' Kabbalah,' which is chiefly a treasury of ancient Semitic arcane knowledge, esoteric thought and angelic lore. That is has been abused by black magicians I am open to confess ; but so have the Scriptures. In the Middle Ages it was misconceived by popular European opinion as a compendium of sorcery and forbidden knowledge, In this absurd superstition the Luciferians recognized their opportunity. Sedulously they fostered the opinion that it was a cyclopedia of the darkest magical belief, in order that the full odium of sorcery might fall upon the Jews and be diverted from themselves. I am neither pro- nor anti-Semite, any more than I am pro- or anti-negro. Like the vast majority of my fellow-countrymen, and especially of my fellow-Scotsmen, I only desire to see justice done to an important section of humanity, which first conferred upon it the greatest boon in the world—the knowledge of the fellowship of man with God, the knowledge that it is possible for man to commune with God and walk in His companionship.

Where is the centre of this hidden Satanist power situated ? After long consideration of this question I believe it to be somewhere in the Baltic region. My reasons for so thinking are as follows : Anciently Courland, the southern portion of the old Baltic Provinces, is known to have been the chief centre of Black Magic and Luciferian activity in Europe, and signs of its survival there are not lacking. From that quarter seems to have emanated the Satanism which dominated the early Bolshevist propaganda and acts of outrage. From Reval, in Esthonia, was directed the outburst of Satanism and necromancy which visited Helsingfors in Finland in the year 1931, and which was absurdly attributed to influences from London. Reval was the birthplace and early home of Alfred Rosenberg. Danzig is also unquestionably a centre of Satanist conspiracy. It is the headquarters of Dr. Karl Hans Fuchs, the propagandist of the Nazi claims to ' the Polish corridor ' and a prominent member of an occult school in Germany whose name I withhold because it might give pain to numerous people in this country who believed it to be an agency for good until it betrayed their principles. This arcane institution was certainly in touch with Rosenberg, who actually received from it some of the arguments he employed in his *Mythus*. Some years ago Dr. Fuchs called upon me while visiting Edinburgh, with a view to eliciting some information on the subject of the Atlantean question, when I had no difficulty in arriving at definite conclusions respecting the disingenuous character of his general attitude to things arcane. Danzig is also the residence of the Satanist, Felix Dodeleben. I may not dogmatize on this matter. I can only say that such evidence as I possess seems to point to the Baltic region as the present seat of the Luciferian nucleus.

In conclusion, I believe the present war to have been brought about by the influences of the Luciferian power upon the Nazi regime and especially, through that of its servant Alfred Rosenberg, upon Adolf Hitler. The eastward-looking tendency of Rosenberg's foreign policy was, sooner or later, bound to eventuate in war and in the nihilist spirit of his writings, in which the Teutonic warrior is glorified above all other types. the intention to precipitate war is manifest. The monstrous cruelty with which the Nazi programme has been carried out is in itself significant of Satanist origin and intention.

Rosenberg has, of course, made a pretence of following in the philosophic wake of writers like H. S. Chamberlain, Lagarde, and others who proclaimed excellencies of German culture. What, in effect, is this German ' culture ' ?

Years before the Nazi Party went into the business of blood and iron the Nordic theory, developed by men who had not even a'prentice acquaintance with Anthropology, the Science of Race, was not only discredited, but had been laughed out of court. Even in the days of its inception Professor Max Müller, himself a German, jeered at it unmercifully, and Dr. H. F. K. Gunther, who was presumably predisposed to the Teutonic myth, felt himself bound to declare that Germany was only about 60 per cent Nordic, and that only some 5 or 6 per cent of Germans were purely Nordic at that.

But it finally received its death-blow when, in 1926,

Professor F. H. Hankins, in his *Racial Basis of Civilization,* revealed its contradictions and its absurdities. These disclosures, however, instead of putting a period to the claims of the advocates of Teutonism, merely spurred them on to the commission of fresh imbecilities. Official German anthropologists dare not at their peril cease from defending it and sought new interpretations for it.

Most people are aware nowadays of the general claims and significance of the Nordic theory. Roughly speaking, it postulates the racial superiority of people with blond hair and blue eyes. People like Herr Hitler, Herr Alfred Rosenberg, and Dr. Goebbels, none of whom is fair, appear to have an almost pious respect for their golden-capped opposites.

This great race of amber-haired, azure-eyed champions, we are told, originated somewhere in Northern Europe and quickly began to show its superiority to ordinary humanity by butchering and enslaving it. Once the dominating power in our continent, it shortly revealed mental and spiritual qualities so much above the capacity of the darker or brown-haired races who had previously existed there as to appear to them almost as semi-divine. 'The qualities of the German character,' are, we are told, eternal, ' and everything else must be subordinated to them.' Those who don't agree, or who can't fit into the philosophic and cultural scheme of the fair-haired supermen, are classed as ' abjects,' ' Mongolians,' ' mongrels,' or ' submen.' All that is great in Art or Science proceeds from the blond Nordic alone.

Not only in more recent years have Åberg, Reinesth, and Petsch quite cruelly displayed the historical fallacy and the æsthetic absurdity of this nauseous and maladroit exhibition of racial caddishness, but the whole record of Science and Art simply clamours against it. More than fifty years ago the French anthropologists, with sly humour, clearly demonstrated that the populations on either side of the Franco-German frontier for a distance cf fifty miles each way, were substantially of the same type, and with Gallic glee broadcast the horrid truth that although about 60 per cent of North German children were of fair

colouring up to the age of twelve, the great majority of
them took on a much darker hue in later life—that in a
word, Nordic blondness was about as constant a quality as
the Nordic word.

Germany is, in fact, full of dark people, most of them very
much swarthier than ourselves. Are all of these ' abjects,'
' sub-men,' and if so, what are their reactions to the soft
impeachment ? Are all these millions, in the good time of
the Golden-haired, to be bred out of existence or concentrated in separate enclaves? The bare fact is that the
racial composition of the German people is practically the
same as that of the rest of Europe, only the several elements
which go to its making are mixed in slightly different proportions—and that holds good for all of us.

And is the Germanic race so vastly superior in the
things of the mind, heart, and soul to other European
races? I am aware that thousands of people in this
country fatuously believe it to be so, especially in a
professor-ridden Scotland, where an inexpensive and thinly-
coated university system has splashed a veneer of rough-
cast culture across the frontages of artisan education.
Yet the triumphs of British Literature utterly put into the
shade the mightiest essays of German letters, as any international critic of experience and honesty would be compelled to admit. Neither in the spheres of poetry, the
drama, or the novel has Germany approached even our
secondary standards. As regards fine painting we are easily
victorious. Only in the musical art does the Teuton
outsoar us. And, at the risk of shocking most people, I
have to confess that I have found most of his music
commonplace, pedantic, and somnolently pompous when
compared with the rhapsodies of Hungary, the imaginative
wonderland of Russian music, or the fairyland of French
melody. To me the whole body of it reeks of the contra-
puntal grammarian and the *kapellmeister*.

In more than one science we have beaten Germany on
her own ground. The Scotland of a century and a half
ago re-created German philosophy, a process it sadly
required, and in folklore the despised Englishman has shown
the German plodder to be a mere myth-dredger. In the

sphere of practical science—electricity, engineering, ship-building—the other European races have demonstrably outstripped Germany, who has merely mimed their efforts. In the roll of invention hers is a secondary place indeed. The German is notoriously a deplorable colonist. The German Press is a living example of what a public Press should not be. Only in town-planning and a sense of the value of amenity does Germany surpass us. The great mass of her noble Nordic population is dejected, brow-beaten, and amazingly sycophantic to its fantastic rulers.

It is the defeated, truculent spirit of the inferiority complex which has driven Germany to accept the doctrine of racial superiority. By repeating the legend of that superiority after the manner of Coué, she hopes to convince herself of its veracity—a superstition at once so gross and so reminiscent of man's adolescence that a free and well-ordered people can only regard it with amusement tinged with a compassionate contempt.

One day—and that day is not far distant—the whole buckram myth of Germany's intellectual superiority will collapse and shrivel beneath the blows of genuine criticism —a criticism which can only arise when the Anglo-Saxon peoples recover from their credulous surprise at the enormity of the insolent claims she has put forward.

Civilization is not merely progress in the material sense, it resides not only in art and literature, but in the deep-founded joy of goodness, of righteousness, of justice, of mercy. At its best, it is the fruit of the knowledge of man's fellowship and co-operation with his Creator. For the future, a genuine spiritual re-awakening must herald the new day of man's rebirth. The dark and evil powers which have so long afflicted him with woe and political dissension must be tracked down and destroyed as hunters track and slay the ferocious beasts of the jungle. Then, and then only, will he be enabled in true serenity of mind and soul to approach his great and destined task—the discovery of that path which will lead him to communion with the Divine—the true Magic, the surpassing and sacred Art of all Arts, the quest mysterious and ineffable.

This mystical and serenely beautiful island of ours awaits

the ordeal of battle with the legions of a hell-inspired multitude with manly calmness and resolution. In God is our trust. The certainty of His triumph is ours. Tried we may be to the uttermost, but victory is assured by our alliance with Divine virtue and destiny. The Hand that shaped this planet will not permit its deflection into the dark and terrible paths which lead to the abyss. Britain, the sea-borne Ark, bearing the symbols of truth and righteousness, will pass unscathed through the tempest to the haven of that victory which is peace.

REFERENCES

1. See the Rev. John Raymond Crosby, in *The Living Church* for 2 March, 1929 ; Montague Summers, *A Popular History of Witchcraft,* 1937, Chapter V, Part II, *passim* ; Charles Godfrey Leland, *Aradia, or the Witches of Italy,* 1899. *passim.*
2. For the allegations of this sort see A. E. Waite, *Devil Worship in France, passim,* who ridicules the notion.
3. For a list of those religions which entertain a dualistic belief see my *Introduction to Mythology,* pp. 145-6.
4. Montague Summers, *The History of Witchcraft and Demonology,* pp. 14–27.
5. Mansel, *Gnostic Heresies, passim.*
6. See my *Legends and Romances of Brittany,* pp. 173–80 ; M. A. Murray, *The God of the Witches,* pp. 191 ff. ; Summers, *The Geography of Witchcraft,* pp. 389–96.
7. Raoul Gineste, *Louis Gaufridi et Magdeleine de la Palud,* 1904.
8. Desmaret, *Histoire de Magdelaine Bavent,* 1652.
9. M. Summers, *Popular History of Witchcraft,* pp. 169 ff.
10. M. Summers, *Popular History of Witchcraft,* pp. 254–7.
11. P. 291.
12. E. S. Bugge, *Home of the Eddic Poems.* (Translated by Schofield, Grimm Library.) 1899.
13. Charles Mackay, *Extraordinary Popular Delusions,* Vol. II, p.111.
14. C. Mackay, op. cit., Vol. II, p. 162 f.
15. See *Malleus Maleficarum.* Translated into English. Edited by Montague Summers. (The Church and Witchcraft series.)
16. J. J. Görres, *Die christliche Mystik,* 1836–42.
17. For the ritual of Witchcraft, see M. A. Murray, *The Witch-cult in Western Europe,* 1921, and her *God of the Witches,* N.D., *passim.*
18. See his essay ' Goethe and the Faust Legend,' in *The Atlantis Quarterly,* Vol. I, No. 2, pp. 70 ff.
19. *Les Sectes de Sociétès Secrètes,* p. 100.
20. Pp. 157 ff.
21. Pp. 178–9.
22. N. H. Webster, *Secret Societies and Subversive Movements,* p. 153
23. N. H. Webster, op. cit., pp. 230–1.
24. Op. cit., pp. 235 ff.
25. *Essai sur la Secte des Illumines,* Vol. II.
26. P. 117.

27. Op. cit., pp. 245–6.
28. Eckert, *La Franc-Maçonnerie dans sa veritable signification,* Vol. II, p. 125.
29. Webster, op. cit., pp. 255–7.
30. P. 30.
31. Pp. 258–65.
32. Webster, op. cit., p. 266.
33. Heiden, *History of National Socialism,* p. 5.
34. *Mythus des 20 n. Jahrhunderts, Berlin,* 1930, p. 2.
35. Op. cit., pp. 22–3.
36. Op. cit., pp. 81–2.
37. Op. cit., pp. 202–3.
38. Op. cit., p. 204.
39. Op. cit., p. 79.
40. Op. cit., p. 145.
41. Op. cit., pp. 247, 294.
42. *The Racial Conception of the World.* (Friends of Europe Publication, No. 37.)
43. *Hitlerism, Why and Whither.* (Friends of Europe Publication, No. 22.)
44. Rosenberg, *Mythus,* pp. 603–4.
45. Op. cit., p. 616.
46. Yarker, *Arcane Schools,* p. 132.
47. Bergmann, *Die 25 Thesen der Deutschreligion,* p. 84.
48. Kusserow, *Das Nordische Artbekenntnis,* pp. 12–13.
49. Rosenberg, *Mythus,* p. 606.
50. Bergmann, op. cit., p. 21.
51. Op. cit., p. 12.
52. Op. cit., p. 9.
53. Op. cit., p. 10.
54. Op. cit., p. 23.
55. Op. cit., p. 46.
56. Op. cit., p. 66.
57. Op. cit., p. 67.
58. Op. cit., p. 71.
59. *Outline of a German-Nordic Religion,* p. 8.
60. Op. cit., p. 142.
61. Op. cit., p. 23.
62. Op. cit., p. 32.
63. See my article 'The Neo-Pagan Movement in Germany,' in *The Quarterly Review* for July, 1940.
64. *The Creed of the Nordic Race.* (Friends of Europe Publication, No. 41.) Foreword.
65. René Fülöp-Miller, *The Mind and Face of Bolshevism,* pp. 190–1.
66. A. E. Waite, *The Secret Tradition in Freemasonry,* I, pp. 296, 370, 415.
67. A. E. Waite, op. cit., I, p. 289.
68. *Le Pouvoir occulte contre la France,* pp. 273–8.
69. *Recherches politiques et historiques sur l'existence d'une secte revolutionnaire,* p. 2.
70. Op. cit., p. 521.
71. *A History of National Socialism,* pp. 44–6. (The italics are mine—L. S.)
72. Op. cit., p. 67.
73. Op. cit., pp. 264, 269.
74. Rauschning, *Hitler Speaks,* p. 57.

CPSIA information can be obtained
at www.ICGtesting.com
Printed in the USA
BVHW061448240221
600996BV00009B/324